Cooking for

Andy Ennis

recipes edited by Joan Nielsen

A FIRESIDE BOOK Published by Simon & Schuster

To Little Miss
and
To my parents, for setting such a beautiful table, where I learned to enjoy life

F

FIRESIDE
Rockefeller Center
1230 Avenue of the Americas
New York, NY 10020

Copyright © 1997 by Andy Ennis
All rights reserved,
including the right of reproduction
in whole or in part in any form.

FIRESIDE and colophon are registered trademarks
of Simon & Schuster Inc.

Designed by Bonni Leon-Berman

Manufactured in the United States of America

1   3   5   7   9   10   8   6   4   2

Library of Congress Cataloging-in-Publication Data
Ennis, Andy.
Cooking for Cher / Andy Ennis ; recipes edited by Joan Nielsen.
p.   cm.
"A Fireside book."
Includes index.
1. Cookery.   2. Low-fat diet—Recipes.   3. Cher, date.
I. Cher, date.   II. Nielsen, Joan.   III. Title.
TX714.E55   1997
641.5′638—dc21   97-19697
CIP
ISBN 0-684-81493-5

Acknowledgments

Cooking for Cher is a result of my passion for cooking and the tireless efforts of many people who generously contributed their time, love, and talent. Being a first-time author has been a challenging yet very gratifying experience, and it is only through my work with all of these great people that this project could have come to fruition. I have learned lessons from each of you, no matter how big or small, that have left an indelible impression upon me. I would like to offer my heartfelt thanks to all of you for giving me the inspiration and support I needed throughout this entire process.

To Cher, for leading me on this incredible journey and having the patience to put up with my preoccupation. You were my boss; you have *become* my confidante, therapist, healer, comedian, friend, and second family—you are all woman! Your strong beliefs in healthy eating and enjoyment of my cooking have been the inspiration for this book. Thank you for giving me the opportunity to pursue my passion.

Cher's assistants: To Deb Paull, my savior; I am still praying to St. Anthony. For your unwavering strength, "there must be a solution" attitude, and encouraging words, thank you, the martini and cold pasta are on me. To Jennifer Ruiz, for your persistence and honest feedback; and to Darby "Do That Dance" Bowen and Nathalie "Deanna Troy" Morgan, for constantly keeping me entertained.

And Warren Grant, Renee Walters, and Gayle Lillie.

Special thanks to Bill Sammeth, always making the seemingly impossible become possible. I am indebted to you for getting me the answers and being there when things were really tough.

And Billy's assistants: Liza Joseph and Annie Caccavo, for your good humor in rationalizing our strange predicaments; and Joshua Anderson, for your diligence in seeing things through.

My family is my lifeblood. Their guidance, encouragement, love, and unfaltering support provide the harmony and inspiraton in my life. To my mother, Pat, who graced me with the delicious inspiration of her cooking; my father, Don, who taught me high standards, to "bend with the breeze," and make the kitchen table a grounding place to discuss life's accomplishments and challenges; and Ellen and Dennie; Connie, Paul, and "Mr. Apple Pie" Lucas; Rich, Debby, and Mathew; and Nancy; whose advice, valuable feedback, and big appetites guided me in the right direction to complete this cookbook. And to my grand-mother, Claire, who instilled in me an appreciation for the food that is grown in our world and to "never waste food." My thanks for sharing a very big heart for what is important in life.

Sydny Miner, my even-keeled and scrupulous editor at Simon & Schuster, deserves a big round of applause. Her gentle persistence, good suggestions, and attention to detail have turned my labor of love into a book I'm really proud of. I appreciate her patience with a first-time author having a full-time job in the midst of it all. And thanks, Syd, for reminding me to take "deep breaths" at times when I thought I couldn't, and teaching me to appreciate some of my accomplishments.

Also at Simon & Schuster: Cherlynne Li, whose art direction, vision, and tedious work on the photographs has made this book look so special; as well as Bonni Leon-Berman, whose vital design role achieved clarity and usability; Katy Riegel (design director for Fireside); Ani Go, production manager; Elaine Magee, for the nutritional analyses; Toni Rachiele (copyediting supervisor), for shepherding the book through copyediting and proofreading; Jane Mollman, the copyeditor; Monica Gomez, Sydny's assistant, for the thankless task of sending my work through, cheerfully; and any others at Simon & Schuster who have contributed their efforts to this book.

I am grateful to my literary agents, Maureen and Eric Lasher, for their advice and nurturing over the years in getting this project off the ground.

I am forever indebted to Christine Roberts for getting the ball rolling. Your perseverance and infectious smile made getting over that first hurdle a real pleasure. Also in the beginning, my thanks to Jane Carroll, Joan Nielsen, and Hilary Dole Klein.

To my ever-inspiring mentors—it is through my experiences with them that I draw culinary masterpieces each and every day: Patrick Clark, Lydia Shire, Bernhard Mueller, Donald Wressel, Nancy Silverton, and Jeanne Jones. A special thanks to Christian Chavanne, who introduced me to Cher through the spa cuisine cooking that he so passionately taught me. Christian, my hat's off to you, Fredna, and your children for making such a difference in my life.

Chazz Palminteri, through his rousing words, one late night in the kitchen, which instilled in me the importance of the individual and to never let go, at any cost, the dreams that we each envision; for that is the human spirit that makes each of us unique. Thank you for believing in me, but more important, for inspiring me (through your amazing talent) to believe in myself.

Barbara Johnson, my eighth-grade English teacher, for giving me the building blocks to write well; your continued encouragement motivated me throughout the writing of this book.

Jennifer Black, my ever-faithful, determined recipe tester. Thank you for all the late nights you worked in creating desserts and testing my recipes. Thanks to Paul Rodriguez for computer support, Rebecca Ruiz for nutritional counseling, and Georganne La Piere-Bartylak and Stephen Miny for the tedious and thankless task of rummaging through years of photographs to find just the right ones. You're the best! Paul Shapiro and Douglas Sutter, whose keen photographic expertise and advice were invaluable. And special thanks to Harry Langdon for gracing this book with the cover photograph.

To my ever-loyal family of tasters, whose faith in my cooking and heartfelt accolades keep me going every day: Cher, of course, and Georgia Holt, Georganne La Piere-Bartylak, Ebar Bartylak, Chastity Bono, Laura LaMastro, Christy Bono, Elijah Blue Allman, Grandma Lynda (posthumously), Grandpa Charlie, Joe DeCarlo, Robert Camilletti, Stephen Miny, Paulette and Duane Betts, Maria Villatoro, Jose Lemus, Pat Piburn, Teri Scott, Adrienne Angel, Evelyn Halus, Nancy Sill, Debbie Green, Laurie Solomon, and Richard Stark.

And to my incredible friends, who have understood and withstood, for their unrelenting support during my long silence. They always asked, "How's the book coming along?" even when they knew I might be too busy to answer. I have missed their wonderful ways and can't wait to see them all again: Gregory Balaban, Bobi Thomson, Judy Post Roll, Marty Bosworth, Cat Gwynn, Douglas Sutter, Ross Harmon, Meridith Gold, Lynn Grigsby, Bryce Romig, Mary Robertson, Jillian Newman, Christine Roberts, Jeanie Danis, Harris and Debi Gellman, Janet Bussell, Katie Kinnerk, Benny Bacolores, Rita Dever, and Deb Kennedy.

All who know Jessica Ruiz understand what an incredibly lucky man I am. She was the one closest to this project, the one who understood what I was going through when few others did. Thank you from the bottom of my heart.

Contents

Foreword

I've always loved flavorful food.

My mom is from the South, so when I was growing up, we ate lots of chicken, vegetables, and fruit, big fresh salads, beans, and corn bread. We always had a big pitcher of iced tea in our kitchen. My mother didn't like coffee, so I never really acquired a taste for it, and to this day I may have only two cups of coffee in a year.

As a child, I ate really slowly (I still do), and my mom would get furious because it took me so long to finish my meals (I think I picked that up from my father). We didn't have much money, so we didn't eat a lot of meat, and as a result, I have never really cared for it. (Even now I can't stand the idea of sitting down to a meal of a big slab of red meat.) At my house we seldom serve red meat, so, of course, my kids think it's a treat.

When I was about ten, my mother found what I believe was the only health-food grocery store in the San Fernando Valley and decided that she was going to completely change the way she cooked. She came home with all kinds of weird (!) food like nuts, raisins and dates, sprouts, and peanut oil. At that time (in the mid-fifties), when you thought of nuts, you thought of the Planter's Peanut Man, but my mom would bring home *raw* nuts, and we always had a big bowl of them on our kitchen table. Even though I liked the taste of them, I thought they were nerdy, and that my mom was crazy for going to this stupid thing called a health-food store and getting *carrot* juice.

Of course, when I was a teenager I wanted to eat all the awful crap that all teenagers eat. Since I was always *really* skinny, I didn't think about my insides, not until I became an adult—it was then that I hired my first "health-food chef," Marcia Stone. Marcia was great and her food was fresh, low-fat, and absolutely delicious. She was with me for three years but wanted to leave to have a baby and could no longer keep the same schedule. At one point around this time, I spent a few days at the Golden Door Spa, shaping up to film my *I Found Someone* video. While there, I met a chef I liked named Christian Chavanne, and I asked him to recommend the best chef he knew. This turned out to be Andy, who came and "auditioned" for me by cooking his (now famous) Moroccan Chicken Stew and Couscous. I loved it (and him!) and he has been with me ever since.

I love tasty, spicy food, and even though I watch how much I eat, and eat low-fat food, I never feel deprived. If you start with good food, you can change your habits without a lot of suffering. For example, there was a time when I drank a six-pack of Dr Pepper a day. When I realized that it was actually the cold liquid and bubbles that I liked, I substituted a sparkling mineral water, then slowly replaced that with regular bottled water. Now I keep a bottle of still water with me constantly. I also used to drink whole milk; now I drink nonfat milk, and couldn't drink a glass of whole milk if you put a gun to my head. It's too rich; it tastes like cream. Once you change the way you eat, your tastes actually change.

You've got to eat nutritiously in order to have your body work for you. You know, we're more careful about the fuel we put into our cars than the fuel we put into our bodies. We know what kind of fuel our car needs to run most efficiently—unleaded or super-premium—yet we put all kinds of unhealthy things into our bodies and think that they won't affect us, but they do. You can't get away with putting bad things into your body, whether chemicals or foods. There's no reason to eat badly today. There are so many ways to have the things you love: You can have food that tastes fabulous and is really good for you at the same time. It's not one or the other.

I know where I'm tempted to go wrong, and sometimes I go through periods of not eating so well, though my idea of not eating well may not be the same as everybody else's idea of not eating well. I confess that I have this terrible chocolate addiction. It's been my nemesis since I was a young woman. I don't smoke, I don't do drugs, so chocolate is a vice I can tolerate. I just watch how much I eat, and in what form: chocolate nonfat yogurt versus chocolate ice cream, for example.

I'm so happy to feel physically fit, and I expect to feel that way until I die. I know that a lot of it has to do with the way I eat. I also keep up a pretty strenuous exercise routine, four or five days a week, an hour to an hour and a half a day. To maintain that kind of schedule, my body needs lots of nutritional building blocks; without them I couldn't build muscle. My food is important to me, even though I don't cook. I *can* cook (I actually cook well), but my heart isn't in it. I keep strange hours, and it's hard for me to stick to a regular schedule, especially if I'm working all day or all night. I can't eat just before I'm going on stage, or before I rehearse and record; you can't do this kind of work feeling full. So sometimes I forget to eat, then all of a sudden I'm starving! I've got to be careful that I don't just grab something sweet, especially if I'm stressed out. I love Andy's food so much that I even take him with me when I'm on tour or on a movie set.

Cooking for me is a challenge; I'm very difficult to please, and Andy's often feeding a house full of people. And when I'm really hungry, I've been known to run down the hallway and say, "Andy! Feed me or I'll kill you." Then we both laugh. He's so creative, and is constantly coming up with ways to take a recipe my family loves and cut down on the fat and calories. He can change that recipe and make it taste absolutely great and still be healthful. Like the other night he made a cobbler and that's all anyone talked about: "Did you get the cobbler?" "No, I missed the cobbler." "Oh, you poor thing! You didn't get the cobbler!" The cobbler talk went on for days. People in my house would be in tears if Andy stopped cooking!

In this book, Andy wanted to give you some of his favorite recipes, including some of my family recipes that he's made healthier. He also has included a special ten-day meal plan and shared some of the special memories he has of our family, and the food that made those memories. Like Chastity's spinach, my ambrosia, and my mom's stuffing, which we have every Christmas. If you cook from these pages, you'll be making food that tastes delicious, but you won't have to feel guilty for eating it. So I hope you enjoy the book half as much as I've enjoyed Andy's cooking the recipes for me. I know you'll really love the food.

God bless!

Introduction

In the late sixties I was still romping around the house in my one-piece pajamas with the padded feet, tugging at my mother's apron strings as she cooked, while my sister Nancy sang "I Got You Babe" in front of the bathroom mirror, holding a blow dryer as an imaginary microphone. She was the entertainer in our family, but never did I think that twenty years later I would be cooking for the ultimate entertainer, Cher.

Since we grew up in a large family, our lives were shaped more around events at the kitchen table than anywhere else. Food was the magnet for nurturing conversation, love, and caring. Every day, food became more of a passion for me as my mother, an accomplished gourmet cook, introduced me to the wonderfully satisfying world of cooking.

Each meal was a time to remember. My father had a vast Michigan oak kitchen table custom-made for us, and around it we would savor my mother's cooking. There were the festive holiday family reunions, where my grandfather would bring out his homemade elderberry wine from the creaky stairs of his basement below. And on weekends my father would take us out to Chicago restaurants to splurge on Bookbinder soup heady with sherry, Greek cheese flaming in ouzo, or fresh pasta in an Italian neighborhood. These experiences trained my palate and gave me the desire to create great food.

At age nineteen, I turned my academic focus toward a career in my lifelong passion, that of cooking. I received my formal training at the Culinary Institute of America, which not only deepened my curiosity about the culinary world but also suggested what tremendously hard work and exciting challenges lay ahead for me. It was at the end of that rigorous training that I discovered I had gained an unthinkable (for me) thirty pounds—surely not from the hollandaise, charcuterie, and three-egg omelets every day! This additional weight, gained primarily from classically prepared food loaded with butter, heavy cream, and egg yolks gave me the desire to experiment with healthier forms of cooking. I wanted to cook food that was high in flavor and low in fat.

In the eighties, Americans were fast becoming aware of the importance of fitness and healthy eating, and I wanted to be a part of what I knew would be more than just a passing trend. After interning with chef Patrick Clark in New York City, I accepted an apprenticeship with spa chef Christian Chavanne at the Four Seasons Resort and Club in Dallas. He gave me my first opportunity to develop my own low-fat style of cooking. It was Christian who introduced me to Cher.

At the time, the Four Seasons Hotels were at the forefront of the industry in providing "alternative cuisine" for their guests who wanted to reduce their intake of calories, fat, cholesterol, and sodium without compromising taste. In Dallas, Christian and I spent several months testing various healthful cooking methods —such as grilling, steaming, and poaching—and cooking preparations such as marinating with fresh juices, using vegetable purées as thickeners, and finding alternative ingredients that allowed us to decrease the calories and fat in recipes while retaining taste and texture. Our resulting menu items tempted guests with such flavorful creations as blue corn crab enchiladas, vegetable bouillabaisse, and mesquite-grilled duck and spa mole sauce.

In 1987, I transferred to the Beverly Hills Four Seasons Hotel to work with renowned chef Lydia Shire. Her emerging "new American cuisine" was a creative blending of seasonal American products with diverse ethnic influences. Lydia's incredible ingenuity and teaching ability challenged me to add a whole new dimension to my low-fat cooking style through the use of ethnic spices and unusual combinations of ingredients. As her *chef de partie* (lead hot-food chef), amid the buzz of Hollywood agents and actors, I prepared such uncommon delights as seared tuna with olive pappardelle and barbecued lobster surrounded by Chinese potstickers.

At the same time, Cher was looking for a personal chef knowledgeable about low-fat cuisine, and she heard about me through Christian Chavanne. By then I had been cooking spa food for over five years. The prospect of cooking for Cher came at a perfect time in my professional life, because it gave me the opportunity to apply my low-fat cooking techniques to someone whose lifestyle demanded it. I met with Cher to discuss her dietary needs and to prepare samples of my cooking. She couldn't believe how delicious my food tasted! At this point, we both knew that if I accepted the job, which I gladly did, it would be the perfect situation for both of us.

Through my cooking experience and my own philosophy of cooking healthfully, I immediately understood what was important to Cher. Her emphasis had always been on keeping fit, working out, and healthy eating. This meant focusing on grains, poultry, seafood, fruits, and vegetables. She had a sophisticated palate and wanted food that was highly flavorful. Cher wasn't shy about experimenting with different spices and foods; she simply wanted no-frills meals that were good for her and tasted great.

The most creative part of my job begins with planning each day's menu. Cher leaves a great deal up to me, so I get most of my inspiration from daily trips to the grocery, farmers' market, or fishmonger. The freshest foods available dictate what I use in the meals for the day. I buy armfuls of the freshest fruits, vegetables like baby greens and field-ripened tomatoes, fragrant herbs, and often, fresh seafood or poultry. A rustic loaf of Nancy Silverton's La Brea Bakery bread usually rounds out my shopping list.

Once I arrive at Cher's home, I can always count on two things—the house is usually in a state of frenzy and the first words out of Cher's mouth are "Andy! Feed me or I'll kill you." In a short amount of time, I'll prepare her favorite Salade Niçoise with grilled fresh tuna, or Barbecue Chicken Burgers and Dill Coleslaw. It's all smiles from there (and I've just saved my life!).

Dinners at Cher's house range from ethnic dishes such as Moroccan Chicken Stew and Couscous to simple Turkey Chili and Mexican Corn Bread, or sophisticated Salmon en Papillote and Chilled Asparagus with Balsamic Vinaigrette. All day, people walking in or out of the house inevitably end up in the kitchen. In the afternoon, Cher will come in, lean against the countertop, and pick at anything I'm chopping on the cutting board. (For years I've had visions of mistakenly nicking her finger as she's sampling!) By evening, wonderful aromas are wafting throughout the house, attracting family and friends. One by one, they wander into the kitchen to taste the cucumber raita I will serve with the lemony Tandoori Chicken Brochettes. Or they will try the oddly named Frankies, which are not even remotely similar to frankfurters but are an Indian version of a burrito. My version is filled with potato and cauliflower, spiced with pungent curry powder, and topped with a thick, sweet mango chutney. I have a great audience and the food is the star.

I have now been Cher's personal chef since 1989, bringing my culinary knowledge, talent, and creativity full circle and employing it on a one-on-one basis. I may find myself suddenly cooking for a cast of characters that includes Michelle Pfeiffer, Roseanne, Richie Sambora, Daryl Hannah, Chazz Palminteri, director Paul Mazursky, Winona Ryder, Christina Ricci, and Don Johnson. Cher is surrounded by amazing friends and talent, but to me, there is no one as tough, hard-working, and multifaceted as she.

My food has played an integral part in fueling the seemingly endless accomplishments of this inexhaustible woman: Over the years, I have set up and cooked in eight new homes, gone "on the road" in her "Heart of Stone," "Love Hurts," and now "It's a Man's World" music tours, for which Cher had a special traveling kitchen road case designed specifically for my equipment and ingredients. I've been on location for the filming of her music videos, like *If I Could Turn Back Time,* the Cher fitness video, the movies *Mermaids* and *Faithful,* and her riveting performance on HBO of *If These Walls Could Talk.*

Cher and I have been discussing this cookbook for a long time. It contains her favorite recipes that I cook frequently, recipes we thought other people would like to be able to cook in their own homes. With these recipes we have combined the qualities most important to Cher (and me) in one style of cooking —healthy, low-fat, great-tasting food. Most people don't realize that Cher rarely eats in restaurants, because she thinks she has the best food in Los Angeles at home. She has loads of friends and loves to invite them to her house to eat in what she calls "the best restaurant in town."

One of the great things about this cookbook is that I've brought my restaurant cooking knowledge to the home cook. All my recipes have been cooked for Cher over and over again in home kitchens, using home equipment and utensils and easily found ingredients. I hope you take as much pleasure in preparing and serving these recipes as I have had in creating them and sharing them with you.

Cher's Pantry
Essential Food Items for Healthy Eating

Let's face it, one reason many of us grab junk food or fast food is that we don't have any better options in our cupboards or refrigerator at home. Sure, a burger and fries taste great every once in a while, but as our lives get busier and more hectic (at least mine does), it only follows that we will increasingly look for a quick fix when we're on the run, at the expense of our health. Here is a solution.

One of the things I do at Cher's home to keep everyone eating well is to have a varied and well-stocked pantry. People, including Cher, are always coming and going, with different and sometimes conflicting schedules, so it is important to have a good foundation of healthy food on hand. No time? A once-a-week trip to the grocery store is all it really takes to keep good food around you. Believe me, the time spent in shopping will be well worth it. You will feel better and be more productive, because you're nourishing your body!

With the following food staples, creating a meal is possible at any time of the day with the least amount of effort. If I prefer a particular brand, I've noted the name because I think it has outstanding characteristics, but you can substitute what is readily available to you. Whether Cher is just rushing out the door (with little plastic bags of food that I've packed for her) or a group of friends have just arrived, there is always an array of good, healthful foods from which I (or they) can choose.

PANTRY STAPLES
CEREALS, GRAINS, NUTS, AND LEGUMES
Cereals: Irish oats, old-fashioned oatmeal, shredded wheat, baked (low-fat)
 granola

Grains: long-grained white rice, brown rice, basmati rice, wild rice, stone-ground cornmeal, popcorn, whole-grain breads

Baked whole-grain crackers, whole-grain rice cakes, unsalted pretzels, baked tortilla chips, corn tortillas

Pasta: angel hair (capellini), penne, macaroni shells, couscous (Near East)

Noodles: lasagna, egg, udon; or fresh yakisoba/chow mein

Raw nuts: almonds, sunflower seeds, sesame seeds (good sources of protein, but limit intake because they are high in fat)

Legumes: pinto, black, and kidney beans, garbanzo beans (chickpeas), black-eyed peas, Great Northern white beans, split peas, lentils

FRESH PRODUCE

Fruits: apples, papayas, cherries, strawberries, raspberries, pears, grapefruit, oranges, lemons, limes

Vegetables: high-fiber vegetables like broccoli, red and green cabbage, carrots, and brussels sprouts. Others to include: asparagus, avocado, beets, cucumbers, eggplant, green beans, mushrooms, potatoes, snow peas, turnips, winter squashes (like acorn, butternut, spaghetti), yams, yellow squash, zucchini

Washed and dried salad greens (which can be bought already prepared and bagged)

Green leafy vegetables: spinach, mustard greens, Swiss chard, kale

Fresh herbs: basil, dill, parsley, cilantro, rosemary, mint

Fresh chiles: jalapeño, serrano, poblano, Anaheim green

Fresh salsa

Onions, red onions, shallots, garlic

FRESH POULTRY, MEATS, SEAFOOD, AND DAIRY

Poultry: skinless chicken breasts, sliced roasted turkey, lean ground turkey and chicken, turkey sausage

Meats: lean cuts of beef (like beef chuck), lean ground beef, port tenderloin

Seafood: halibut, sole, orange roughy, swordfish, albacore tuna, shrimp, scallops, salmon

Dairy: nonfat milk, low-fat buttermilk, evaporated skim milk, nonfat yogurt, low-fat cottage cheese, light sour cream, egg whites

Cheese: low-fat or fat-free ricotta, part-skim or fat-free mozzarella, grated cheddar, thin sliced provolone, feta, soy "cheese"

SEASONINGS, SPICES AND CONDIMENTS . . . THINGS TO SPICE UP LOW-FAT FOODS

Seasonings: all-purpose low-sodium seasoning blends (like Spike, Veg-it, or Mrs. Dash), curry and tandoori spice blends (Sharwood's), garlic salt blends, chili spice mix, ranch dressing mix (Hidden Valley Ranch), blackened Cajun spice blend (Chef Paul Prudhomme's magic seasoning blends—blackened redfish magic), crab boil spices (Zatarain's), crystallized ginger, lemon pepper

Spices (to name a few essential ones): salt, sea salt and kosher salt, black peppercorns, cinnamon, crushed red pepper, cumin, chili powder, basil, Greek and Mexican oregano, Italian herb seasoning, fennel seed, caraway seed, celery seed, thyme, curry powder, Beau Monde

Condiments: Dijon mustard, low-sodium soy sauce, hot sauce, barbecue sauce (like Woody's Cook-in' sauce barbecue concentrate, for grilled foods or as a recipe ingredient, or Johnny D's Hogwash barbecue baste for grilled chicken), Major Grey's Indian mango chutney, teriyaki sauce (Soy Vay sesame Veri Veri teriyaki marinade and sauce), Pickapeppa sauce, prepared horseradish, reduced-fat mayonnaise, enchilada sauce

CANS AND JARS

All-fruit preserves, apple butter, applesauce

Fruit, such as pineapple, packed in water or natural juice

Vinegars: balsamic, white wine, rice wine, sherry wine, raspberry

Oils: extra-virgin olive, dark toasted sesame, canola, safflower, peanut, vegetable oil cooking spray

Low-sodium chicken broth, vegetable broth, and beef broth (preferred over powdered or bouillon cubes)

Unsweetened natural-style (with the oil floating on top) peanut butter (unhomogenized)

Water-packed albacore tuna

Canned tomatoes and tomato purée

Sun-dried tomatoes (dried, not the ones packed in oil)

Low-fat coconut milk

Miscellaneous: grape leaves, capers, green chiles, Mexican-style hominy, beans

Olives: kalamata, Spanish green, oil-cured black

HEALTHY BEVERAGES

Fresh-squeezed fruit juices and smoothies, vegetable juices

Caffeine-free tea, herbal tea, no-sugar fruit-flavored iced tea

Decaffeinated coffee (Swiss or water-washed method)
Sparkling water

QUICK, LOW-FAT SWEETS

Frozen fruits: grapes, bananas, mangoes, or cherries
Dried cherries, cranberries, raisins, and currants
Hot chocolate mix (prepared with nonfat or low-fat milk), good-quality
   Dutch-process cocoa powder
Nonfat or fruit-sweetened chocolate fudge sauce (Wax Orchards' classic fudge)
Licorice (Cher's favorite nonfat sweet)
Nonfat frozen yogurt or sorbet

WHAT YOU WON'T FIND

Alcoholic beverages (for drinking)
Caffeinated beverages, soft drinks, or diet sodas
Large amounts of sugar, fructose, or corn syrup (it throws off the body's
   metabolism)
Whole milk, processed cheese, and high-fat hard cheeses
Canned vegetables
Fried snack foods: corn chips, potato chips, tortilla chips
Ice cream

CHER, ASTRONAUT

I have always told Cher she would make a great astronaut, because whenever she leaves the house, I pack healthy snacks for her to take along in little plastic bags or Tupperware containers. Even if you're not an international star, it is a great way to get through a busy and hectic day without having to grab junk food along the way.

Planning ahead is really quite simple, and it is the key to eating healthier food. Packing a few simple snacks—an apple, some nuts, low-fat granola, yogurt, low-fat cottage cheese, sliced turkey, hard-boiled eggs, or baked crackers—will make your day, and your body, run much more smoothly. Try being an astronaut for a day! (Of course, the space suit is optional.)

Andy's Kitchen Equipment
Indispensable Gadgets That Eliminate Time and Grief

Working for Cher over the years, I have set up and outfitted countless kitchens for her. We have moved into eight new homes, equipping each of them, not to mention movie locations, music tour venues, tour buses, and hotel rooms. Wherever we travel, I pack many of these items into a kitchen road case (Andy's traveling kitchen) that is ready to fly anywhere at a moment's notice. This is the essential kitchen equipment that I couldn't function without in preparing the various recipes in this cookbook.

COOKWARE AND BAKEWARE

Heavy-duty pots and pans with lids, in various sizes (I use Calphalon): Pans with an aluminum core will conduct heat most evenly and efficiently.

Nonstick omelet (8-inch) and sauté (10- and 12-inch) pans: Especially useful in cooking low-fat foods that would ordinarily stick without the use of oil. It is recommended that they not be used over extremely high heat, though, or the nonstick finish will burn.

Nonstick wok: Very useful cookware designed for stir-frying without excessive amounts of oil.

Cast-iron skillet: For high-heat cooking, well-seasoned cast iron is excellent in browning foods. When generously heated, cast iron will also have nonstick properties, thus eliminating the need to use large amounts of oil in cooking. Also excellent for baking corn bread.

Heavy-duty baking sheets (cookie sheets): I use baking sheets for a multitude of cooking uses: roasting potatoes, baking chicken kebobs, or broiling seafood. Heavy-duty baking sheets are best for high-heat conditions, because they do not have as much of a tendency to warp and they heat more evenly. I use insulated baking sheets for baking cookies.

Glass baking dishes, in various sizes

Muffin tins

Collapsible steamer insert: Fits to almost any size pot or pan; for steaming vegetables, wontons, and the like.

Metal round springform cake pan
Ovenproof bakeware: For baking desserts like flans and soufflés
   Ceramic ramekins (low sides and shallow, 5 ounces)
   Glass custard cups (6 ounces)
   Soufflé cups (high-sided and deep, 5 to 6 ounces)
   Soufflé dishes (high-sided and deep, 1½ to 2 quarts)

FOOD PREPARATION APPARATUS

Mandoline: A piece of equipment, with different attachments, that is used to slice vegetables uniformly into different shapes and sizes
Salad spinner: Used to dry off leafy greens, such as lettuce or spinach, after rinsing
Mortar and pestle: For grinding and pulverizing whole spices, herbs, and other foods into a finer consistency, thus releasing more of their aroma and flavor; similar to what a coffee grinder does to coffee beans
Peppermill
Hand juicer
Stainless-steel box grater: For grating vegetables or cheese
Hand-held potato masher
Stainless-steel or plastic colanders: For draining foods and preparing fine-sieved breadcrumbs
Mixing bowls, in various sizes

MECHANICAL APPLIANCES

Food processor (my preference is Cuisinart): To chop or purée food
Blender (I use Krups): For puréeing soups, preparing dressings, blended drinks (like smoothies), crushing ice, and other jobs
Electric hand mixer: For mixing batters, whipping egg whites, preparing whipped potatoes

UTENSILS

Good-quality knives (I use Henckels), the single most important group of tools in the kitchen:
   Large chef's knife (8- or 10-inch blade with forged handle)
   Boning knives (flexible or rigid blade for cutting around bones)
   Paring knife (3- to 4-inch narrow blade, for trimming vegetables and other small tasks)
   Sharpening steel (very important in maintaining a fine edge on sharp knives)
   Whetstone or honing stone (essential in sharpening very dull knives)

Meat mallet/tenderizer: For thinly pounding poultry and meat into a uniform thickness

Citrus zester: A hand-held kitchen tool with small, sharp teeth that, when pulled across the surface of an orange or lemon, create thin strips or zest of the outermost peel.

Stainless-steel whisks: For mixing salad dressings or whipping eggs

Long-handled tongs and metal spatula: Ideal for barbecue grilling. The long handles keep hands at a safe distance from flames when you are cooking food on a barbecue grill.

Rubber spatulas, in various shapes and sizes: I use these for a multitude of kitchen tasks: scraping bowls and blenders, removing food mixtures from the food processor, or folding ingredients together. Also ideal for use with nonstick cookware.

Nonstick spatulas: Ideally suited to turning foods in nonstick cookware, which would otherwise be damaged by rigid metal spatulas.

Ice-cream scoop

MISCELLANEOUS

Baking parchment: Ideal for lining baking sheets and cake pans to prevent sticking

Zip-top plastic bags: Excellent for storing rinsed and dried produce, especially lettuce and spinach

Foil, wax paper, and plastic wrap

Foil muffin cups

Metal or bamboo skewers

Food storage containers: To store prepared, refrigerated foods

Self-locking glass jars: To store coffees, cocoa, nuts, or dried fruits

Starters

Cher's Ranch Salad

Salad makes 5 to 6 side servings, 2 to 3 main-course servings
Dressing makes 1 cup

*A*lthough it's just a simple green salad, Cher's ranch salad is one of my most frequently requested dishes. Tender Bibb lettuce and assorted chopped vegetables are dressed in a flavorful, creamy ranch dressing that uses low-fat yogurt as its base. As a chef, I am somewhat embarrassed when I describe to people how simple this dressing is to make—only two ingredients and, yes, a package of store-bought ranch mix! You'd think a chef would be a bit more original, but Cher loves this low-fat concoction because it gives her the feeling of being indulgent when, in fact, it's not fattening at all.

This salad is wonderful by itself, or it makes an excellent accompaniment to many of the meals I suggest in this cookbook. The salad ingredients listed are what I use most often, but don't be restricted; any of your favorite seasonal vegetables are fine. The ranch dressing can also be used as a dressing over poached salmon or seafood salad, or when the crowds arrive, as a dip for vegetable crudité platters.

CHER'S RANCH DRESSING:
  8 ounces plain nonfat yogurt
  2 tablespoons light sour cream
  4 teaspoons (half of a 1-ounce packet) Hidden Valley Ranch original
    ranch party dip
SALAD:
  1 large head butter, limestone, or Bibb lettuce, leaves washed, dried,
    and torn into bite-size pieces (about 10 cups)
  $^1/_2$ avocado, peeled, pitted, and cut into $^1/_2$-inch cubes
  $^1/_2$ cucumber, halved lengthwise and sliced (about 1$^1/_4$ cups)
  2 stalks celery, washed and thinly sliced
  $^1/_2$ red bell pepper, seeded and thinly sliced
  $^1/_3$ cup thinly sliced red onion (optional)
  Coarsely ground black pepper

To prepare the dressing: In a small mixing bowl, combine the yogurt, sour cream, and ranch seasoning mix. Using a whisk, mix until all of the ingredients are fully incorporated and the dressing is smooth. Refrigerate until needed. (The dressing will keep, covered and refrigerated, for up to 1 week.)

To prepare the salad: Combine the lettuce, avocado, cucumber, celery, red bell pepper, and red onion, if using, in a large mixing bowl. Toss lightly with $^1/_2$ cup of the dressing. Taste and add more dressing as needed. Season with a grinding of black pepper.

VARIATIONS AND SUGGESTIONS:
This dressing makes a perfect low-fat base for many other salad dressing possibilities.

Green Goddess Dressing: In a blender or food processor fitted with a metal blade, mix the above dressing ingredients and add $^1/_2$ of a peeled and pitted avocado. Blend a few seconds until smooth.

Blue Cheese Dressing: In a blender or food processor fitted with a metal blade, mix the above dressing ingredients and add 1 tablespoon of blue cheese. Blend until smooth.

Mexicali Dressing: In a blender or food processor fitted with a metal blade, mix the above dressing ingredients and add $^1/_3$ cup of salsa, 1 tablespoon of chopped cilantro, and 2 teaspoons of cumin. Blend until smooth.

NUTRITIONAL ANALYSIS PER SERVING (1 small salad with dressing):
Calories: 80 • Protein: 3.76 grams • Carbohydrates: 7.93 grams • Fiber: 2.82 grams • Fat: Total: 3.69 grams • Saturated: 0.769 gram • Cholesterol: 1.4 milligrams • Sodium: 250 milligrams

SELECTING FRESH ASPARAGUS

When selecting asparagus, use your senses of touch, smell, and sight. The tips should be tight, without any heavy musty odor, while the stalks should feel firm, not spongy, and snap easily when bent between your fingers. Any stalks that appear brown or silvery gray, not completely green, are overmature and will be woody.

Chilled Asparagus with Balsamic Vinaigrette

Salad serves 6
Vinaigrette makes $^1/_2$ cup

*T*his is a delightfully simple yet elegant salad that takes advantage of the springtime bounty of tender asparagus. I serve it as a starter at many of Cher's dinner parties, and since I am usually quite busy at serving time, it is reassuring to know that this salad can be prepared in advance and held in the refrigerator.

BALSAMIC VINAIGRETTE:
    1 tablespoon Dijon mustard
    1 tablespoon white wine vinegar
    2 tablespoons balsamic vinegar
    2 tablespoons finely minced shallots
    1 teaspoon lightly chopped capers
    2 tablespoons chopped parsley
    Pinch of sugar
    2 tablespoons extra-virgin olive oil
SALAD:
    2 teaspoons salt
    3$^1/_4$ pounds fresh asparagus, tough ends removed
    1 roasted red bell pepper (see page 37), cut into $^1/_4$-inch julienne
        strips
    2 tablespoons chopped parsley

To prepare the vinaigrette: Combine the mustard, vinegars, shallots, capers, parsley, and sugar in a small bowl. Whisking continuously, slowly drizzle the oil into the mixture until the vinaigrette attains a thick and homogeneous consistency. Refrigerate.

To prepare the asparagus, make an ice bath by filling a large bowl or pan with ice and cold water. Bring 3$^1/_2$ quarts of water and the salt to a boil in a large pot.

Using a vegetable peeler, peel the bottom half of the asparagus stems below the tips (this will remove any woody, fibrous parts and result in tender stalks after cooking). Tie the stalks with string into four individual bundles. Blanch in the boiling water until tender but still very green, about 3 to 4 minutes. Stop the cooking process by submerging each bundle of asparagus in the ice bath. Drain, remove string, and refrigerate the asparagus, loosely covered with moist paper towels.

To serve, place equal amounts of asparagus, in six individual bundles, on salad plates. Spoon equal amounts of the vinaigrette over each portion. Place several strips of roasted red bell pepper on top and sprinkle with chopped parsley.

NOTE:

For a more substantial salad, make a bed of torn Bibb lettuce leaves on which to serve the asparagus.

NUTRITIONAL ANALYSIS PER SERVING:
Calories: 100 • Protein: 4.75 grams • Carbohydrates: 12 grams • Fiber: 4.35 grams • Fat: Total: 5.15 grams • Saturated: 0.714 gram • Cholesterol: 0 • Sodium: 87.5 milligrams

Blood Orange and Avocado Salad

Salad serves 4
Vinaigrette makes about $1/4$ cup

everal years ago, on a trip to Greece, Cher raved about a blood orange salad with olive oil and cracked black pepper. My version is a striking display of crimson blood oranges and fanned-out avocado slices, drizzled with raspberry vinaigrette and extra-virgin olive oil. This glorious salad is quick and simple, yet elegant. On many occasions I have substituted regular oranges when I could not find blood oranges—though maybe we should all just go to Greece!

RASPBERRY VINAIGRETTE (see Note):
2 tablespoons raspberry vinegar or red wine vinegar
$1/4$ teaspoon grated orange zest
1 tablespoon fresh orange juice
$1/2$ teaspoon honey
2 teaspoons extra-virgin olive oil
1 teaspoon walnut oil

SALAD:
1 semifirm avocado
4 medium Bibb lettuce leaves, or more, washed and dried
4 blood oranges (or navel oranges), peeled and cut into $1/4$-inch rounds
$1/2$ pint fresh raspberries (optional)
2 teaspoons extra-virgin olive oil
Cracked or coarsely ground black pepper

To prepare the vinaigrette: Combine the vinegar, orange zest, orange juice, and honey in a small bowl. Whisk in the olive oil and walnut oil. Refrigerate.

To fan out the avocado, quarter it from the stem end to the top and peel the skin off each section. Using a small paring knife, gently pry each section away from the pit. Lay each wedge on a cutting board and slice it very thinly lengthwise, starting about $1/2$ inch from the stem end (this will keep the slices joined). With the palm of your hand, gently press down on each wedge until the slices spread out evenly. Transfer the fanned wedges to a plate.

To assemble the salad, place a Bibb lettuce leaf on each of four salad plates, spread out the orange slices overlapping one another, lean a fanned avocado wedge up against the oranges, and scatter a few raspberries, if using, around the plates.

Sprinkle each salad with about 1 teaspoon of the vinaigrette, $1/2$ teaspoon of the olive oil, and a generous grinding of black pepper. Pass the remaining vinaigrette on the side.

NOTE:

If you are short on time, try using one of the good-quality raspberry vinaigrettes, like the one from Silver Palate, that are on the market now.

NUTRITIONAL ANALYSIS PER SERVING (with approximately 1 teaspoon vinaigrette): Calories: 203 • Protein: 2.59 grams • Carbohydrates: 22.3 grams • Fiber: 4.45 grams • Fat: Total: 13.5 grams • Saturated: 1.95 grams • Cholesterol: 0 • Sodium: 6.88 milligrams

COOKING IS A SYMPHONY!

My brother once gave me a great analogy for cooking. He suggested that each recipe is like an orchestra, and the ingredients are the individual instruments. In every recipe there are the high-note ingredients and the low-note ingredients, and when they are all combined, they create music!

It really makes sense, because in cooking, just as in an orchestra, if any one thing is left out or too many things are put in, all you have is a clash. Cooking is a balance. Take, for example, my blood orange and avocado salad: The tangy citrus is a high note, but when combined with the heavier taste of avocado, the salad becomes a nice balanced blend of ingredients. Experiment with your tastes and you will soon discover that cooking, like life, is a symphony just waiting to happen.

HOW TO ROAST BELL PEPPERS

Preheat an oven broiler and position a shelf close to the heat source. Place the bell peppers on a baking sheet or foil. Broil the peppers, turning often, until their skins blister and blacken. Alternatively, you may place the peppers directly over an open flame on a gas stove until charred, turning with long-handled tongs.

Place the charred peppers in a paper bag or covered container and allow them to steam about 10 minutes, which will complete the cooking process and make it easier to remove the charred skins. With a paring knife or by hand, peel off the charred skin, core the peppers, and discard the seeds. (Do not rinse the peppers in water.) Cut the peppers into whatever size pieces are needed for your recipe.

Greek Tomato-Feta Salad

Salad serves 6 to 8
Vinaigrette makes about $^1/_2$ cup

ustic, earthy flavors star in this combination of summer tomatoes, roasted peppers, Greek olives, and salty feta. The contrasting colors of deep-red tomatoes and pale-green artichokes studded with white feta cheese make this salad a beautiful presentation. It is imperative that the vinaigrette be put on at the last minute or the salad will become watery. Serve with grilled slices of crusty bread if you want a more substantial appetizer.

GREEK VINAIGRETTE:
$^1/_4$ cup balsamic vinegar
1 tablespoon Dijon mustard
$^3/_4$ teaspoon minced garlic
$^1/_4$ cup chopped parsley
$^1/_4$ teaspoon crushed dried oregano
3 tablespoons extra-virgin olive oil
Salt
Freshly ground black pepper

SALAD:
10 to 12 medium tomatoes (about $3^1/_4$ pounds), halved crosswise, squeezed to remove seeds and juice, and cut into large cubes
2 roasted red bell peppers (see page 37), cut into 1-inch squares
1 roasted yellow bell pepper (see page 37), cut into 1-inch squares
1 hothouse cucumber, peeled, seeded, and cut into 1-inch cubes (about 2 cups)
1 can (14 ounces) artichoke hearts packed in water, rinsed, drained, and halved
$^1/_2$ cup kalamata olives, pitted and cut into slivers
6 to 8 Bibb lettuce leaves, washed and dried, to line plates
$^1/_2$ cup crumbled feta cheese (about 2 ounces), for garnish
Chopped parsley, for garnish

To prepare the vinaigrette: Combine the vinegar, mustard, garlic, parsley, and oregano in a small bowl. Whisking continuously, slowly drizzle the oil into the mixture until the vinaigrette attains a thick and homogeneous consistency. Season with salt and pepper to taste. Refrigerate.

Place the tomatoes in a colander to drain any excess juices. In a large bowl, combine the roasted peppers, cucumber, artichoke hearts, and olives.

Just before serving, add the tomatoes to the bowl containing the salad ingredients. Gently mix with about two-thirds of the vinaigrette until evenly coated. Taste, and season with additional salt or pepper if needed.

To assemble the salad, line individual plates with a Bibb lettuce leaf. Spoon equal amounts of the tomato salad onto each plate and sprinkle with the crumbled feta cheese and chopped parsley. Serve, passing the remaining vinaigrette on the side.

NUTRITIONAL ANALYSIS PER SERVING (including dressing but not including any salt added to taste):
Calories: 213 • Protein: 6.51 grams • Carbohydrates: 26.5 grams • Fiber: 8.30 grams • Fat: Total: 11.3 grams • Saturated: 2.92 grams • Cholesterol: 8.33 milligrams • Sodium: 335 milligrams

Spicy Hummus

Makes 3 cups

*A*ummus is a Middle Eastern chickpea paste with subtle lemon and garlic overtones. I serve it many different ways in Cher's home. For company, I serve hummus as a dip in the center of a vegetable crudité platter that often includes Greek olives and warm pita bread. Other times it is the central theme of a light lunch, with grilled vegetables, mixed greens, and sliced blood oranges with fresh mint. However you serve it, you will find this filling, protein-rich hummus very satisfying.

> 2 cans (15½ ounces each) chick-peas (garbanzo beans), rinsed and
>   drained
> 2 tablespoons defatted tahini or sesame butter (pour off any
>   accumulated oil floating on top)
> 1 tablespoon minced garlic
> ½ cup fresh lemon juice
> ¼ teaspoon crushed red pepper
> ⅛ teaspoon cayenne
> ¼ teaspoon salt
> Freshly ground black pepper
> 3 tablespoons chopped parsley

In a food processor fitted with a metal blade, mix all of the ingredients except the parsley with ½ cup water. Process a minute or so until the mixture is very smooth.

Add the parsley and process a few seconds until it is incorporated. Serve at room temperature or chilled.

VARIATIONS AND SUGGESTIONS:

Hummus and Grilled Vegetable Sandwiches: Hummus is a delicious addition to sandwiches. On summer days, I often grill red bell peppers and Japanese eggplant, then spread hummus on grainy bread or a baguette and place the warm grilled vegetables on top. A light, satisfying lunch in a snap!

Hummus-Stuffed Squash Blossoms: Another attractive and elegant presentation: You can stuff hummus into fresh squash blossoms, available from mid to late summer. If you are fortunate enough to have a vegetable garden with zucchini or yellow squash, this is a great way to use up the overabundant blossoms.

Simply rinse the blossoms inside and out. Place hummus into a pastry bag fitted with a plain tip. Squirt about 2 tablespoons of hummus into each blossom and, presented nicely on a platter, they're ready to eat—perfect for a summer picnic in the park.

NUTRITIONAL ANALYSIS PER SERVING ($^{1}/_{2}$ cup):
Calories: 213 • Protein: 8.4 grams • Carbohydrates: 36.3 grams • Fiber: 6 grams • Fat: Total: 4.5 grams • Saturated: 0.6 gram • Cholesterol: 0 • Sodium: 529 milligrams

Dill Coleslaw

*T*his began with Cher's family recipe and her secret ingredient—
pineapple. I added a new dimension by reducing the fat and
adding lots of fresh parsley and dill. This coleslaw is always a big
hit at barbecues or summer luncheon parties. For busy party schedules, this can be
made a day in advance: Keep the cabbage mixture separate from the dressing and
combine the two at the last minute.

COLESLAW:
1 medium green cabbage (about 2¹/₂ pounds)
2 medium carrots, peeled and grated
¹/₂ cup chopped parsley
¹/₃ cup snipped fresh dill
1 can (20 ounces) crushed unsweetened pineapple, well drained

COLESLAW DRESSING:
¹/₂ cup light, reduced-fat mayonnaise
¹/₄ cup plain nonfat yogurt
3 tablespoons Dijon mustard
2 tablespoons sugar
2 teaspoons caraway seeds
¹/₄ teaspoon celery seeds
¹/₄ teaspoon freshly ground black pepper
1 tablespoon sweet pickle relish

Cut the cabbage lengthwise into eighths. Cut out the core from each wedge, then slice the wedges thinly crosswise.

Combine the sliced cabbage, carrots, parsley, dill, and pineapple in a large serving bowl. Cover with plastic wrap and refrigerate.

Mix together all of the dressing ingredients in a small bowl. Chill until needed.

Just prior to serving, add the dressing to the cabbage mixture. Toss well to coat thoroughly. Cover and refrigerate if you must, but the coleslaw is at its best if eaten immediately.

NUTRITIONAL ANALYSIS PER SERVING (1 cup):
Calories: 163 • Protein: 3.49 grams • Carbohydrates: 26.9 grams • Fiber: 4.1 grams • Fat: Total: 6.04 grams • Saturated: 1.1 grams • Cholesterol: 0.138 milligram • Sodium: 306 milligrams

Black-Eyed Pea Salad

*B*lack-eyed peas have an earthy, almost nutlike flavor that is a balanced contrast when paired with this sharp mustardy vinai-grette. Perfect as a first course salad or in addition to a vegetarian meal, these black-eyed peas also make a wonderful accompaniment to Chicken Rollatini with Sun-Dried Tomatoes (page 112), Fajita Skirt Steak (page 129), or Grilled Tuna and Papaya-Mint Salsa (page 82).

SALAD:

- 1 pound (about 2³/₄ cups) dried black-eyed peas, or 3 bags (11 ounces each) fresh
- 2 teaspoons salt
- ¹/₃ cup minced red onion or shallots
- ³/₄ cup finely diced red bell pepper
- ³/₄ cup finely diced yellow bell pepper
- ¹/₃ cup chopped parsley

DIJON VINAIGRETTE:

- 3 tablespoons Dijon mustard
- ¹/₄ teaspoon salt
- ¹/₄ teaspoon freshly ground black pepper
- 2 teaspoons minced garlic
- ¹/₄ cup white wine vinegar
- 2 tablespoons extra-virgin olive oil

Sort and rinse the dried black-eyed peas in a colander, removing any foreign matter or stones. Put the peas and enough water to cover them by at least 3 inches into a large pot. Bring to a boil, then skim off any foam that may rise to the top. Add the salt, reduce the heat, and simmer, covered, 40 to 45 minutes, until the peas are tender but still maintain their shape. Drain. Gently spread the peas on a baking sheet to allow them to cool. Alternatively, if using fresh black-eyed peas, cook according to package directions, or in boiling salted water until soft yet still maintaining their shape, usually 10 to 15 minutes. Allow to cool.

To prepare the vinaigrette: Combine the mustard, salt, pepper, garlic, and vinegar in a small bowl. Whisking continuously, slowly drizzle the olive oil into the mixture until the vinaigrette is thick and homogeneous.

In a large bowl, combine the black-eyed peas with the red onion, red and yellow bell pepper, parsley, and the vinaigrette. Stir to coat thoroughly. Adjust seasonings if necessary with additional mustard, salt, or pepper. Serve at room temperature or chilled.

NUTRITIONAL ANALYSIS PER SERVING:
Calories: 211 • Protein: 5.82 grams • Carbohydrates: 35.2 grams • Fiber: 8.41 grams • Fat: Total: 5.84 grams • Saturated: 0.802 gram • Cholesterol: 0 • Sodium: 211 milligrams

Cher's Ambrosia

Makes 9 cups; serves 10 to 12

This is a rather well-known recipe, but a family favorite that I just couldn't resist putting in this cookbook. On the eve of every Thanksgiving and Christmas, Cher and Chastity assemble this salad. They always prepare it ahead of time and refrigerate it, to allow the marshmallows to "melt" into the mélange of fresh fruit, resulting in a creamy, angel-light concoction. Try it again and you'll remember why you loved it the first time.

> 2 cups fresh orange segments (about 10 medium oranges), all
>   membrane removed and any juice collected
> 2 cups fresh Ruby Red grapefruit segments, all membranes removed
>   and any juice collected (about 3 large grapefruits)
> 2 cups nonfat or low-fat sour cream
> 1 1/2 cups shredded sweetened coconut
> 1 bag (10 1/2 ounces) miniature marshmallows
> 1/2 cup chopped walnuts

In a large bowl, combine the orange and grapefruit segments, along with all the accumulated juice, the sour cream, and the coconut. With a large spoon or rubber spatula, gently mix the ingredients until the sour cream is smooth and coats the fruit segments. (Do not worry if some of the fruit begins to break up into pieces.)

Add the marshmallows and walnuts and gently stir all of the ingredients until they are fully combined. Refrigerate the salad in a covered plastic or glass container for at least 2 hours or preferably overnight, to allow the marshmallows to dissolve into the salad. Before serving, gently stir or fold the ambrosia to incorporate the airy dissolved marshmallows. Serve in individual ramekins or cups.

VARIATIONS AND SUGGESTIONS:
For a slight visual and flavor variation, sometimes Cher adds a spoonful of my Cherry-Lemon Cranberry Sauce (page 48) to the ambrosia. This lends a nice tartness to this sweet salad, while giving it a rosy color.

NUTRITIONAL ANALYSIS PER SERVING:
Calories: 339 • Protein: 6.50 grams • Carbohydrates: 62.3 grams • Fiber: 4.25 grams • Fat: Total: 8.92 grams • Saturated: 4.76 grams • Cholesterol: 0 • Sodium: 88 milligrams

Fond Christmas Memories

*C*her has an extraordinary public image, which is all most people get to know, but through my work, I have been fortunate to get to know her personal, human side as well. Few people know how incredibly thoughtful and considerate she can be.

It was our first Christmas in Cher's new Aspen home. The snow was gently falling over this bustling little town, and I had just prepared a bubbling pot of turkey chili in anticipation of the hungry skiers that would soon stomp through the door. But I was unaware that while I was shopping for food earlier in the day, Cher was planning something special for *me*. She had arranged for Christmas lights to be hung on three evergreens standing outside the kitchen window.

At dusk, Cher and her family walked into the kitchen and said, "Merry Christmas, you lucky cook," as they flipped the switch to light up the beautiful stand of trees outside! It was a wonderful surprise and a Christmas gift I'll never forget.

HOW TO ZEST CITRUS FRUITS

Strong-flavored oils lie within the outermost skin of citrus fruits. Citrus zest is often used in recipes where a powerful fruit flavor is desired without using its juice, which would otherwise water-down a recipe.

The best way to get the outermost skin of a lemon, lime, orange, or other citrus fruit is with a zester, a hand-held utensil with sharp teeth. It is pressed against the outer skin of the fruit and pulled down over the surface, producing neat little strands of the skin.

The same result can be achieved with a paring knife, cutting off the outermost skin, removing any white pith (which is bitter), and slicing the thin skins into short slivers.

Cherry-Lemon Cranberry Sauce

Makes 4 1/2 cups

ny of us who have made fresh cranberry sauce know it takes an enormous amount of sugar (and added calories) to sweeten it, so I developed this recipe using the sweetening power of cherry juice, dried cherries, and an artificial sweetener (the only recipe in this book in which I feel it is necessary). This thick, scarlet sauce is an excellent accompaniment to roasted chicken or turkey with Georgia's Corn Bread Dressing (page 167), the Holiday Spice Whipped Yams (page 164), or as an addition to Cher's Ambrosia (page 45). Cher also loves this cranberry sauce over a sweet slice of sponge cake or pound cake for dessert.

2 1/2 cups cherry juice or cherry cider
1/2 cup dried cherries
2 bags (12 ounces each) fresh or frozen cranberries
1 tablespoon lemon zest (see page 51)
1 1/2 teaspoons powdered artificial sweetener (about 6 to 8 packets, 0.035 ounces each)

In a medium-size saucepan, bring the cherry juice and dried cherries to a boil. Add the cranberries, bring back to a boil, reduce the heat, and simmer, uncovered, about 5 minutes. Stir in the lemon zest, remove from the heat, and allow to cool.

Stir in the artificial sweetener when the cranberry sauce is completely cool; otherwise the sweetener's power will be diminished. (The cranberry sauce can be prepared to this point up to 1 week in advance, covered, and refrigerated.)

Serve chilled.

NUTRITIONAL ANALYSIS PER SERVING (1/2 cup):
Calories: 43.9 • Protein: 0.753 gram • Carbohydrates: 11.5 grams • Fiber: 1.56 grams • Fat: Total: 0.13 grams • Saturated: 0.017 gram • Cholesterol: 0.033 milligram • Sodium: 1.37 milligrams

Chilled Shrimp and Cocktail Sauce

Serves 6, about 5 to 6 shrimp per person

An old standby, but a big favorite in Cher's home. I love having this on hand when entertaining, because the shrimp can be pre-pared up to a day ahead, and this affords me more time to prepare other, more complicated dishes. I am always amazed at everyone's reaction to my simple cocktail sauce. It consists of only two ingredients and can be mixed together in an instant! Prepared horseradish, found in the refrigerated section of your grocery store, is the key ingredient to this power-packed sauce.

SHRIMP:
   3 tablespoons salt
   1 box (3 ounces) crab boil spices (in a boiling bag), or 1/3 cup loose
      (see Note)
   1 lemon, quartered
   1/4 cup dry white wine (optional)
   1 1/2 pounds large shrimp in the shell (16 to 20 per pound)

   6 to 8 cups of ice cubes, to cool shrimp
COCKTAIL SAUCE:
   1/2 cup ketchup
   2 1/2 teaspoons prepared horseradish, or more, to desired strength
GARNISH:
   6 to 8 small Bibb lettuce leaves, rinsed and patted dry
   1 lemon, cut into 6 wedges

To prepare the shrimp: Combine about 2 quarts of water with the salt, crab boil spices, quartered lemon, and white wine, if using. Cover the pot, bring to a rolling boil, and allow the spices to infuse for 5 to 10 minutes.

Add the shrimp and cook, uncovered, until the flesh has turned opaque and the shells are a bright pink, about 3 to 4 minutes. (Do not overcook the shrimp or they will become rubbery. Keep in mind that they will continue to cook from their own accumulated heat, even after you drain them.) Drain the shrimp into a colander. If using crab boil spices in a boiling bag, remove and discard the bag at this point. Immediately mix the shrimp with the ice, to cool them quickly and completely.

Peel and devein the shrimp. Refrigerate. (The shrimp can be prepared up to 1 day ahead to this point and stored, covered and refrigerated.)

To prepare the sauce: Combine the ketchup and horseradish in a small bowl. Taste sauce and adjust strength of horseradish by adding more, if desired. It should pack a little punch.

To serve individual portions: Line each of 6 footed goblets with a lettuce leaf, spoon cocktail sauce on top of the lettuce, hang shrimp over the lips of the goblets, and garnish each portion with a lemon wedge. Alternatively, if entertaining a large party, place a small cup or ramekin of cocktail sauce in the center of a chilled, lettuce-lined platter. Neatly arrange the shrimp around the cocktail sauce and garnish with the lemon wedges. In this case, provide toothpicks to spear the shrimp.

NOTE:

Crab boil spices can be found in the spice section or seafood department of most grocery stores. There are two forms available: loose, or in a boiling bag (similar to a tea bag or sachet). Either will work in this recipe.

NUTRITIONAL ANALYSIS PER SERVING:
Calories: 142 • Protein: 23.3 grams • Carbohydrates: 6.8 grams • Fiber: 0.319 gram • Fat: Total: 2.05 grams • Saturated: 0.384 gram • Cholesterol: 173 milligrams • Sodium: 412 milligrams

Oriental Wontons and Dipping Sauce

Makes about 40 wontons; serves 8 as an appetizer,
5 as an entrée

O ne taste of these steamed wontons will transport you directly to the Orient! A filling of ground chicken or shrimp flavored with sesame oil and green onion is neatly wrapped in thin wonton skins. They are steamed and served with an addictive soy and mirin dipping sauce. It is important to steam the wontons as soon as they are assembled, or the moisture from the filling will cause the wonton skins to disintegrate. If you must prepare them ahead of time, freeze the assembled wontons until you are ready to steam them.

These are perfect as appetizers before a meal such as the Stir-Fried Vegetables with Yakisoba Noodles (page 144), Fiery Pepper Shrimp Fried Rice (page 89), or even Grilled Tuna and Papaya-Mint Salsa (page 82). The wontons also make a beautiful main course, when served alongside Oriental Fried Rice (page 174) and Spinach-Carrot Rolls (page 158).

WONTON FILLING:
1¼ pounds ground chicken or minced shrimp
1½ teaspoons low-sodium soy sauce
¼ teaspoon dark sesame oil
1 teaspoon minced garlic
3 green onions, green part only, very thinly sliced (⅓ cup)
1 package (12 ounces) square wonton skins or round potsticker skins (found in the refrigerated or frozen food section of most grocery stores)

DIPPING SAUCE:
½ cup low-sodium soy sauce
1 teaspoon dark sesame oil
Pinch of crushed red pepper
2 tablespoons sweet rice wine (mirin)
¼ cup chopped fresh cilantro
3 cloves garlic, thinly sliced
1 tablespoon thinly sliced peeled fresh ginger

To prepare the filling: Mix together the ground chicken, soy sauce, sesame oil, garlic, and green onions in a small bowl.

Laying out 4 to 6 wonton skins at a time, place a small ball of the chicken filling (about 1¼ teaspoons) in the center of each wrapper. Wet the outside edges of the skin with water and fold opposite corners over the filling, forming triangles (if you are using square wonton skins) or half moons (if you use round potsticker skins), pressing the edges tightly closed.

Combine all the sauce ingredients in a small cup and mix thoroughly. Set aside.

To steam the wontons, bring a shallow amount of water to a boil in a wide, covered pot fitted with a steamer insert, or a bamboo steamer. Fill the steamer tray with the wontons and steam, covered, 5 to 7 minutes, until firm. Arrange the wontons around the edge of a serving plate centered with a small cup or bowl of the dipping sauce. Dip the freshly steamed wontons into the sauce, with chopsticks if you wish.

NUTRITIONAL ANALYSIS PER SERVING (5 wontons):
Calories: 243 • Protein: 20.29 grams • Carbohydrates: 26.43 grams • Fiber: 0.12 gram • Fat: Total: 5.09 grams • Saturated: 1.24 grams • Cholesterol: 49 milligrams • Sodium: 787 milligrams

Soups and Salads

Clear Wonton Soup

Serves 8

t is hard to imagine (in Cher's home, at least) any oriental wontons being left over from a meal, since they're usually eaten as fast as I can make them. But if some do remain, this wonton soup is an almost instant meal for a light lunch or as the prelude to an oriental-style dinner. In any case, I use half of my Oriental Wonton recipe (without the dipping sauce) to prepare steaming bowls of this heartwarming soup filled with mushrooms, green onions, and, of course, Cher's favorite wontons!

WONTONS:
$\frac{1}{2}$ recipe Oriental Wontons (page 51), or 24 leftover wontons,
   without the dipping sauce
SOUP BASE:
$\frac{2}{3}$ cup ($\frac{1}{2}$ ounce net weight) whole dried shiitake mushrooms
1 can (49 ounces) low-sodium chicken broth
1 tablespoon plus 1 teaspoon low-sodium soy sauce
3 thin slices of peeled fresh ginger
4 green onions, green part only, finely sliced at an angle

If you have no leftover wontons, follow the directions for them (page 51), cutting all measurements in half and filling each wonton skin with *only 1 teaspoon* of filling. Steam the wontons as directed. Set aside.

To prepare the soup base: Combine the dried mushrooms and 1 cup of water in a small pot. Over medium heat, simmer the mushrooms 4 or 5 minutes until soft and pliable. Remove the mushrooms and reserve the liquid. Thoroughly rinse each mushroom to remove any sandy grit, then slice thin. Through a fine-meshed strainer or coffee filter, strain the reserved mushroom liquid into a large saucepan. Add the chicken broth, soy sauce, ginger, green onions, and sliced mushrooms.

Bring to a simmer. Add the wontons and gently simmer several minutes until they are heated through. Remove the ginger slices. Ladle the soup into individual soup bowls and serve immediately.

NUTRITIONAL ANALYSIS PER SERVING (3 wontons per serving):
Calories: 127 • Protein: 9.5 grams • Carbohydrates: 12.6 grams • Fiber: 0.659 gram • Fat: Total: 4 grams • Saturated: 0.722 gram • Cholesterol: 29 milligrams • Sodium: 166 milligrams

Spicy Corn Chowder

Serves 6

*his chowder gets its creaminess from puréed corn and potatoes,
without the addition of fattening heavy cream or butter. Chunks
of potato and whole corn are added to give the soup its texture
and body. It makes a wonderful, warming meal on chilly winter days.*

1 tablespoon extra-virgin olive oil or butter
3 cups chopped onions
1 cup diced celery
2 yellow bell peppers, seeded and chopped (about 2 cups)
1 tablespoon minced garlic
4 cups fresh or frozen whole kernel corn
3 cups diced peeled potatoes
1 can (14^1/$_2$ ounces) low-sodium chicken broth or vegetable broth
1 teaspoon sea salt
1 teaspoon dried rubbed sage
Pinch of crushed dried oregano
Pinch of dried thyme
3 tablespoons canned diced mild green chiles, rinsed
1 tablespoon snipped fresh dill, plus 6 sprigs for garnish
^{1}/$_4$ teaspoon Tabasco (optional)
Freshly ground black pepper

Heat the olive oil in a large soup pot over medium heat. Sweat the onions,
^{1}/$_2$ cup of the celery, the yellow bell peppers, and the garlic until softened but
not browned, about 8 minutes.

Add 2 cups of the corn, 1 cup of the potatoes, the chicken broth, 2 cups
water, and the salt, sage, oregano, and thyme. Bring to a boil, reduce the heat,
and simmer, covered, 20 to 25 minutes, stirring occasionally. Purée the corn
mixture very smooth in a blender or food processor fitted with a metal blade, in
as many batches as necessary. (Be careful, when puréeing, not to fill the blender
more than two-thirds full, as the hot liquid may splash out and burn you.
Placing a large kitchen towel over the blender helps in avoiding such an accident.) Return the purée to the pot.

Add the remaining 2 cups corn, the remaining 2 cups potatoes, the remaining
^{1}/$_2$ cup celery, and the green chiles. Simmer until the potatoes and celery are
soft, about 15 minutes, stirring frequently. Remove from the heat.

Stir in the snipped dill. Taste and, if desired, add Tabasco. Stir well and adjust seasoning with salt and freshly ground black pepper to taste. Serve in warm bowls garnished with fresh dill sprigs.

NUTRITIONAL ANALYSIS PER SERVING:
Calories: 218 • Protein: 7.1 grams • Carbohydrates: 43.4 grams • Fiber: 6.92 grams • Fat: Total: 4.38 grams • Saturated: 0.36 gram • Cholesterol: 1.40 milligrams • Sodium: 429 milligrams

Cher's ''Flying'' Exercise Equipment

*C*her will go to great lengths to exercise. It was a cold and rainy day in Boston when Cher, Winona Ryder, and Christina Ricci departed early for an all-day film shoot on the *Mermaids* set. We had just moved into a penthouse apartment there, so I could cook and they could work out in a make-shift gym. I was just returning from the market when I was greeted by several movers who were delivering a huge piece of exercise equipment for Cher; they told me to expect them upstairs shortly.

Meanwhile, I began to fill the apartment with wonderful aromas from a pot of fresh corn chowder, anticipating the mermaids' arrival after their long day. All the while, the movers were trying to shoehorn the exercise equipment into the elevator, but it wouldn't fit. Soon after, Cher, Winona, and Christina arrived home, bone-chilled and weary, and I gladly presented each of them with a mug of steaming chowder. Amid their groans of pleasure, I found their attention drawn to the window. It dawned on me that the movers had never appeared.

Noses pressed to the glass, everyone was in utter disbelief when we saw Cher's gym equipment being hoisted up the side of the building on the window washer's scaffold! It was indeed the strangest delivery ever, but all three were happy to be able to exercise—as soon as they warmed up with my chowder.

Butternut Squash–Apple Soup

Serves 6 to 8

*B*rilliantly orange, this velvety-smooth soup develops a beautiful aroma from pumpkin pie spice, cinnamon, and nutmeg, conjuring up memories of freshly baked apple pie on a crisp autumn day. For a light lunch, follow the soup with Shredded Vegetable Salad with Low-Fat Blue Cheese Dressing (page 69), or for a heartier dinner accompaniment, the Beef Stew and Vegetables (page 125).

> 2 teaspoons butter
> $1^3/_4$ cups diced onion
> 2 teaspoons minced garlic
> 1 butternut squash (about $3^1/_2$ pounds), peeled, seeded, and cut into $^1/_2$-inch cubes (see Note)
> 1 large red delicious, Fuji, or gala apple (about 8 ounces), cored, peeled, and diced
> 1 can ($14^1/_2$ ounces) vegetable broth
> $^1/_4$ teaspoon pumpkin pie spice
> $^1/_4$ teaspoon ground cinnamon
> $^1/_2$ to 1 cup apple juice or water
> $^1/_2$ teaspoon nutmeg (optional)

Melt the butter in a large soup pot. Sauté the onion and garlic over medium heat until softened but not browned, about 5 minutes. Add the squash, apple, vegetable broth, $3^1/_2$ cups water, the pumpkin pie spice, and cinnamon. Bring to a boil, reduce the heat, and simmer, covered, until the squash and apple are soft, 20 to 25 minutes.

Purée the soup in a blender or food processor fitted with a metal blade, in as many batches as necessary. (Be careful, when puréeing, not to fill the blender more than two-thirds full or the hot liquid may splash out and burn you. Placing a large kitchen towel over the top of the blender helps in avoiding such an accident.) Thin the soup, if necessary, with $^1/_2$ cup or more of apple juice. The consistency should be just thin enough to coat the back of a spoon.

Return the puréed soup to the pot and reheat. Serve in warm bowls with a light sprinkling of nutmeg, if desired.

NOTE

It is very important to keep a steady grip on your knife when peeling the hard rind off squash, as the blade of the knife can easily go askew. Try always to cut downward, toward the cutting board, and never hold the squash below the blade of the knife.

VARIATION:

For a slightly different taste, prepare the soup as directed, adding $1/2$ teaspoon of curry powder and omitting the nutmeg.

NUTRITIONAL ANALYSIS PER SERVING:
Calories: 125 • Protein: 2.48 grams • Carbohydrates: 28.1 grams • Fiber: 5.24 grams • Fat: Total: 1.93 grams • Saturated: 0.863 gram • Cholesterol: 3.45 milligrams • Sodium: 312 milligrams

HOW TO SWEAT VEGETABLES

Sweating vegetables, is essentially a way to minimize the use of oil in a recipe. Instead of sautéing in oil, usually for a browned or caramelized effect, sweating is used to soften vegetables where no color or caramelizing is desired. Sauté the vegetables in a little oil, stock, or water, then place a cover on the pot and allow the steam to soften them.

Potato-Leek Soup

Serves 8

ery quick to prepare and versatile enough to serve hot in the winter or icy cold in the summer. Either version will be a big hit.

> 1 teaspoon butter
> 3¹/₂ cups sliced leeks, white parts only, thoroughly washed
> 2 cups sliced onions
> 3 large potatoes, peeled and sliced (about 2¹/₄ pounds)
> 2 cans (14¹/₂ ounces each) vegetable broth
> ¹/₂ teaspoon sea salt
> 1¹/₂ cups nonfat milk or water
> 2 tablespoons finely snipped chives or dill, for garnish

Melt the butter in a large soup pot over medium heat. Add the leeks and onions, cover the pot, and allow the vegetables to sweat (see page 60) for 5 to 7 minutes, stirring occasionally. Do not brown the vegetables.

Uncover the saucepan and add the potatoes, vegetable broth, 1 cup water, and the sea salt. Bring to a boil, reduce the heat, and simmer, covered, until the vegetables are tender, about 25 minutes.

Purée the soup in a blender or food processor fitted with a metal blade, in as many batches as necessary. (Be careful, when puréeing, not to fill the blender more than two-thirds full, as the hot liquid may splash out and burn you. Placing a large kitchen towel over the top of the blender helps in avoiding such an accident.)

At this point the soup may be served hot or chilled, depending on your preference or the weather. If serving it hot, return the puréed soup to the saucepan, add the milk, and heat before serving. If serving the soup chilled, place the puréed soup in a bowl over ice and chill, stirring occasionally to hasten the cooling process. Once it is cool, stir in the milk.

Adjust the seasoning to taste. Serve in soup bowls with a sprinkling of chives or fresh dill.

NUTRITIONAL ANALYSIS PER SERVING:
Calories: 186 • Protein: 6.01 grams • Carbohydrates: 40.1 grams • Fiber: 3.55 grams • Fat: Total: 1.32 grams • Saturated: 0.415 gram • Cholesterol: 2.12 milligrams • Sodium: 615 milligrams

Curried Yellow Split Pea Soup

Serves 6 to 8

Curry powder imparts an exotic aroma and flavor to this yellow split pea and vegetable soup. It is perfect for a brisk fall or winter day or as part of an ethnically inspired meal. Such a meal could begin with the soup, followed by the Spinach-Feta Salad with Apples and Roasted Sunflower Seeds (page 66), and then Tandoori Chicken Brochettes (page 110).

2 teaspoons butter
2 cups diced onions
1 tablespoon minced garlic
1 cup diced carrots
1 cup diced celery
1 bag (16 ounces) dried yellow split peas, picked over
2 teaspoons curry powder
1 can (14^1/$_2$ ounces) vegetable broth or water
^{1}/$_4$ teaspoon salt
Freshly ground black pepper
1 tablespoon finely chopped parsley, for garnish

Melt the butter in a large soup pot. Sauté the onions, garlic, carrots, and celery over medium heat until softened but not browned, about 6 minutes.

Stir in the split peas and curry. Add the vegetable broth, 6 cups of water, the salt, and pepper. Bring to a boil, reduce the heat, and simmer, covered, until the split peas are soft and the soup is thickened, about 1 hour.

Adjust the seasoning with additional curry, salt, or pepper to taste. Serve in warm soup bowls with a sprinkling of chopped parsley.

NUTRITIONAL ANALYSIS PER SERVING:
Calories: 312 • Protein: 20.4 grams • Carbohydrates: 55 grams • Fiber: 8.17 grams • Fat: Total: 2.63 grams • Saturated: 0.952 gram • Cholesterol: 3.45 milligrams • Sodium: 433 milligrams

Pasta Fagioli Soup

Makes about 12 cups; serves 8

A dear friend of mind translated this recipe from an Italian grand-mother in Venice. It is a thick, hearty bean-and-pasta soup redo-lent of fresh rosemary. I prefer using the dried beans here, instead of canned, because the results are so far superior in taste. Nevertheless, I have included instructions using canned as well, since it shortens the cooking time considerably. If using dried beans, remember to soak them at least 8 hours before preparing the soup. Mangia!

1 pound (about 2^1/$_3$ cups) dried Great Northern beans or 4 cans
    (15 ounces each), rinsed and drained
1^1/$_2$ tablespoons extra-virgin olive oil, plus additional (optional) to
    drizzle on servings
2 medium onions, chopped
1 cup chopped celery
1^1/$_4$ cups chopped carrots
3 tablespoons minced garlic
^{1}/$_2$ cup chopped parsley
1 tablespoon chopped fresh rosemary
1^1/$_4$ cups peeled, seeded, and chopped plum tomatoes (about 3)
1 teaspoon salt (^{1}/$_2$ teaspoon if using canned beans)
^{1}/$_2$ teaspoon garlic salt (^{1}/$_4$ teaspoon if using canned beans)
Freshly ground black pepper
^{3}/$_4$ cup uncooked small elbow or salad macaroni
Grated Parmesan cheese (optional)

Sort and rinse the dried beans in a colander, removing any foreign matter or stones. In a bowl, soak the beans for 8 to 12 hours in enough cold water to cover them by at least 4 inches. Drain.

Heat the olive oil in a large soup pot over medium heat. Sauté the onions, celery, and carrots until softened, about 8 minutes. Add the garlic, parsley, and rosemary and continue to cook another 2 minutes.

Add the beans, tomatoes, and 7 cups of water if using dried, soaked beans (5 cups of water if using canned beans). Bring to a boil and then reduce the heat to low. Cover and simmer the beans, stirring occasionally, about 1^1/$_2$ hours for the soaked beans, or 20 minutes for the canned beans, until they are soft and tender.

Season with the salt, garlic salt, and black pepper. Add the raw macaroni and continue to simmer another 15 to 20 minutes, until the macaroni is tender and the soup has thickened considerably. Stir frequently to prevent the macaroni from sticking to the bottom of the pot. Remove from the heat.

At this point the soup will have a very thick consistency. If it is too thick, add some additional water. Adjust the seasoning, if necessary, by adding more rosemary, salt, or garlic salt.

Serve in soup bowls with the Parmesan, if using, and a drizzle of extra-virgin olive oil, if desired.

NUTRITIONAL ANALYSIS PER SERVING:
Calories: 216 • Protein: 11.1 grams • Carbohydrates: 37 grams • Fiber: 7.93 grams • Fat: Total: 3.4 grams • Saturated: 0.550 gram • Cholesterol: 0 • Sodium: 385 milligrams

HOW TO CLEAN SPINACH

Thoroughly washing spinach is critical to the success of your recipes. There is nothing worse than discovering that spinach is sandy after you have already prepared a meal with it!

To clean spinach, discard any leaves that are bruised or yellowed. Wash the spinach leaves in a bowl or sinkful of cool water, stirring to dislodge sand and other debris. Lift out the rinsed leaves, placing them in a bowl or colander, drain the sandy water, and repeat the washing process two or more times to ensure that the spinach is clean and completely free of any grit. Dry the spinach in a salad spinner or on paper towels, then wrap in a damp towel and refrigerate until needed.

HOW TO STEM SPINACH WITHOUT DAMAGING THE LEAVES

For spinach salads or other recipes where only the leaves are desired, it is important to know how to remove the stems without damaging the leaves. Here's a chef's trick: Place the bottom of the leaf upward. With one hand, hold the leaf just above where it meets the stem. With your other hand, grip the stem and gently pull up. The stem should snap just below the leaf; then as you continue to pull, the stringy parts of the leaf should come off with it. The result is tender spinach leaves without any stringy fibers.

Spinach-Feta Salad with Apples and Roasted Sunflower Seeds

Serves 2 or 3 as a main course, 5 to 6 as a starter

*T*his is a wonderful salad in the fall or winter, especially during inclement months when the quality of lettuce is poor. It combines a contrasting blend of tart apples, sharp feta cheese, roasted sunflower seeds, and a sweet-tart vinaigrette.

CITRUS VINAIGRETTE:
> 2 tablespoons Champagne vinegar or white wine vinegar
> $1/4$ teaspoon grated orange zest (see page 47)
> 1 tablespoon fresh orange or grapefruit juice
> $1/2$ teaspoon honey
> 1 tablespoon or more extra-virgin olive oil

SALAD:
> 1 bunch spinach (1 pound), stemmed, thoroughly washed, and dried (see page 65)
> $1/4$ cup shelled, raw, unsalted sunflower seeds
> 1 large Granny Smith or other green apple, unpeeled, cored, and julienned
> $1/2$ cup crumbled feta cheese (about 2 ounces)
> 1 teaspoon orange zest
> Freshly ground black pepper

To prepare the vinaigrette: Combine the vinegar, orange zest, juice, and honey in a small bowl. Whisk in the olive oil. Adjust the taste, if necessary, with additional honey or olive oil. Refrigerate.

Tear or cut the spinach leaves into bite-size pieces, cover loosely with moist paper towels, and refrigerate until ready to use.

In a sauté pan over medium heat, dry-roast the sunflower seeds until golden, 6 to 8 minutes. Toss often to prevent burning. Remove from the pan and allow to cool.

To assemble the salad, combine the spinach, apple, feta cheese, and orange zest in a large serving bowl. Toss lightly with the vinaigrette, then add the sunflower seeds and a light grinding of black pepper. Toss again and serve.

NUTRITIONAL ANALYSIS PER SERVING:
Calories: 305 • Protein: 13 grams • Carbohydrates: 22 grams • Fiber: 6.2 grams • Fat: Total: 20 grams • Saturated: 7.5 grams • Cholesterol: 0 • Sodium: 578 milligrams

Curried Chicken–Wild Rice Salad

Makes 11 1/2 cups; serves 6 to 8 as a main course

I was first introduced to this fabulous recipe by Cher's previous chef, Marcia Stone. Poached chicken, wild rice, currants, and crunchy vegetables are combined with a curry-and-chutney dressing, and the bright-yellow color of the dressing makes an appealing contrast with the black speckles of wild rice, the red pimiento, and the green vegetables. I often prepare this one day ahead; the taste improves over time as all the flavors of the spices marry.

1/2 medium onion, sliced
6 boneless, skinless chicken breast halves (about 2 1/2 pounds), rinsed (see Note)
1 teaspoon curry powder
1/2 teaspoon ground coriander
1/2 teaspoon ground cumin
1/2 teaspoon salt
Freshly ground black pepper
1/2 cup uncooked wild rice
1/2 cup uncooked brown rice

DRESSING:
1/4 cup chopped mango chutney
1 tablespoon curry powder
1 teaspoon ground coriander
1/2 teaspoon ground cumin
1/2 teaspoon turmeric
Dash of garlic salt
1/3 cup red French dressing
1/4 cup light or fat-free mayonnaise
Tabasco, to taste

SALAD:
1 cup diced celery
1/4 cup thinly sliced green onions
1/2 cup chopped parsley
1 jar (4 ounces) pimiento strips, drained
1 can (2 1/4 ounces) sliced black olives, drained
1/4 cup dark raisins or currants
1 cup frozen green peas, thawed

Scatter the onion slices in the bottom of a large, wide pot or dutch oven. Lay the chicken breasts in a single layer on top of the onions. Sprinkle on the curry powder, coriander, cumin, $1/4$ teaspoon of the salt, and the pepper. Add just enough water to cover. Bring to a gentle boil, reduce the heat, and simmer, covered, about 15 minutes, until the chicken is firm. Uncover the pot and allow the chicken to cool in the broth. Drain the poaching liquid and cut the chicken into $1/2$-inch cubes. Set aside.

In a medium pot, combine the wild rice and brown rice with $2^1/2$ cups of water and the remaining $1/4$ teaspoon of salt. Bring to a boil, reduce the heat, and slowly simmer, covered, about 45 minutes, until the rice is tender. Remove from the heat and drain, if necessary. Set aside, uncovered, and allow the rice to cool. Fluff with a fork.

To prepare the dressing: In a large mixing bowl, combine the chutney, curry powder, coriander, cumin, turmeric, garlic salt, French dressing, mayonnaise, and Tabasco. Mix well. Add the chicken, rice, celery, green onions, parsley, pimiento, olives, raisins, and peas. Mix thoroughly. Chill the salad, tightly covered, from 2 to 12 hours to allow all of the flavors to mingle. (The salad can be prepared up to 1 day ahead.)

Serve chilled.

NOTE:

Small to medium-size shrimp can be substituted for the chicken, with all the other ingredients remaining the same.

VARIATIONS AND SUGGESTIONS:

For a stunning presentation, serve the curried chicken in a hollowed-out pineapple shell, with the diced pineapple flesh mixed into the salad. If using shrimp in place of the chicken, try stuffing the salad into papaya halves.

NUTRITIONAL ANALYSIS PER SERVING:
Calories: 354 • Protein: 32.2 grams • Carbohydrates: 39.4 grams • Fiber: 4.64 grams • Fat: Total: 7.64 grams • Saturated: 1.48 grams • Cholesterol: 69.3 milligrams • Sodium: 519 milligrams

Shredded Vegetable Salad with Low-Fat Blue Cheese Dressing

Serves 4 as a main course, 6 to 8 as a starter

*T*he best way to prepare this salad easily is with a piece of kitchen equipment that I consider indispensable—my mandoline (see "Andy's Kitchen Equipment," page 25). You can quickly cut any vegetables into matchstick sizes (short julienne) by sliding the vegetable across a sharp blade. Using a grater can result in watery vegetables, but if you drain them in a colander you can achieve similar results. This salad, with a crispy baguette, makes a perfect summer main course or, in smaller portions, a prelude to dinner.

BLUE CHEESE DRESSING (see Note):
    1 cup (1 recipe) Cher's Ranch Dressing (page 31)
    1 tablespoon blue cheese
SALAD:
    $1/2$ pound broccoli
    4 medium beets (about 1 pound), stems and leaves removed
    4 medium carrots, peeled and cut into short julienne pieces (2 cups)
    3 small yellow summer squash, stems removed, cut into short julienne pieces (2 cups)
    2 small zucchini, stems removed, cut lengthwise and crosswise into short julienne pieces (2 cups)
    $1/2$ pound purple cabbage, quartered, core removed, and shredded into $1/2$-inch slices (3 cups)

To prepare the dressing: Combine the ranch dressing and the blue cheese in a blender. Blend until smooth. Refrigerate in a covered container until ready to use.

In a medium pot, bring 1 quart of water to a boil and, holding the broccoli by its stems, plunge the entire flowering head into the water for only a few seconds, until it is bright green. Refresh under cold running water. Cut the stems off close to the head. Peel the stems and slice into short julienne pieces. Finely chop the florets and place them in a large bowl with the julienned broccoli stems.

Pour out all but about 1 inch of the water in the pot used for the broccoli. Set a steamer insert into the pot. Add the beets and steam 20 minutes (just enough so the skins can be easily removed). Cool, then remove the skins and cut into julienne slices. Put in a small bowl separate from the other vegetables.

To the bowl containing the broccoli, add the carrots, yellow squash, zucchini, and purple cabbage. Chill, covered with a damp towel. (The salad may be prepared ahead to this point.)

To assemble the salad, toss all of the vegetables except the beets with the blue cheese dressing. Mound equal amounts of the dressed vegetables in the center of each plate. Garnish each salad with a scattering of the beets and serve.

NOTE:

Even though this blue cheese dressing is quick to prepare, if you are short on time, a store-bought low-fat blue cheese dressing is a perfectly acceptable substitute.

NUTRITIONAL ANALYSIS PER SERVING (without dressing):
Calories: 116 • Protein: 6.3 grams • Carbohydrates: 24.0 grams • Fiber: 8.29 grams • Fat: Total: 1.43 grams • Saturated: 0.534 gram • Cholesterol: 1.59 milligrams • Sodium: 118 milligrams

NUTRITIONAL ANALYSIS PER SERVING (with dressing):
Calories: 293 • Protein: 22.3 grams • Carbohydrates: 45.4 grams • Fiber: 8.4 grams • Fat: Total: 3 grams • Saturated: 2.3 grams • Cholesterol: 15.6 milligrams • Sodium: 571 milligrams

On the Road

One might think that after eight years of cooking for Cher, things would run pretty smoothly. But when I log upwards of 25,000 miles of travel with her each year, I face some daunting challenges in getting dinner to the table. Whether we are on a music tour traveling on a bus or just stepping off an airplane en route to a film location, there is only one thing I can predict—everyone is hungry.

Advance planning is my salvation. I often get maps of the cities we will be in and then call ahead to locate the markets closest to our destination. My other saving grace is my kitchen road case—like a huge steamer trunk on wheels—which Cher had custom-made for me. This case carries all of my vital cooking equipment—knives, utensils, pots and pans, even appliances—as well as unusual spices and ingredients that I know I probably will not be able to find at a moment's notice. With all of this, plus my own adrenaline, I always seem to produce meals for Cher that keep her happy and looking great.

Italian Chopped Salad

Serves 4 to 5 as a main course, 6 to 8 as a starter

T he ultimate tossed salad—finely shredded lettuce, tomatoes, gar-banzo beans, spicy peperoncini (hot peppers), and just a hint of dry salami are tossed in an Italian vinaigrette. The salami, stud-ded with peppercorns, adds a hearty dimension to this otherwise light salad, although it could be prepared without the salami as well.

ITALIAN VINAIGRETTE (see Note):
   $1/2$ cup Italian red wine vinegar
   $1/3$ cup white wine vinegar
   2 tablespoons coarsely chopped fresh basil
   1 tablespoon crushed dried oregano
   $1/2$ teaspoon fennel seed, crushed in a mortar and pestle
   $1/2$ teaspoon garlic salt
   2 tablespoons extra-virgin olive oil
SALAD:
   2 small heads romaine lettuce, stems removed and leaves washed, dried, and finely sliced $1/8$ inch thick
   1 head iceberg lettuce, quartered, core removed, and leaves washed, dried, and finely sliced $1/8$ inch thick
   1 can ($15^{1}/2$ ounces) garbanzo beans (chickpeas), drained
   1 jar ($15^{1}/2$ ounces) peperoncini (hot peppers), drained, stems removed, and cut into thin round slices
   6 ounces sliced dry salami with peppercorns, sliced into thin julienne pieces
   3 cups cored and chopped fresh tomatoes
   1 cup chopped cucumber
   $3^{3}/4$ ounces grated part-skim or fat-free mozzarella cheese
   Freshly ground black pepper
   Fresh basil or oregano sprigs, for garnish

To prepare the vinaigrette: Combine the red and white wine vinegars, basil, oregano, fennel seed, and garlic salt in a small bowl. Whisk in the olive oil. Refrigerate until ready to use.

In a large bowl, combine the romaine and iceberg lettuce, garbanzo beans, peperoncini, salami, tomatoes, cucumber, and mozzarella cheese. (Because of the large volume of salad ingredients, you may need to toss the salad in several batches.) Whisk the vinaigrette and pour about two-thirds of it over the salad ingredients. Toss the salad until well coated. Taste, add more vinaigrette as needed, and season with a grinding of black pepper.

Mound equal amounts of the dressed salad in the center of each plate. Garnish each with a sprig of basil or oregano placed in the center of each salad, and serve. Pass any remaining vinaigrette separately at the table.

NOTE:

Even though this Italian vinaigrette is quick to prepare, if you are pressed for time, use a store-bought Italian dressing as a substitute, adding a few tablespoons of chopped fresh basil or oregano to the salad.

NUTRITIONAL ANALYSIS PER SERVING:
Calories: 518 • Protein: 22.5 grams • Carbohydrates: 72.5 grams • Fiber: 7.71 grams • Fat: Total: 23.0 grams • Saturated: 7.54 grams • Cholesterol: 38.4 milligrams • Sodium: 300.3 milligrams

Salade Niçoise

Serves 4

*T*his light, refreshing salad is a meal in itself. The grilled tuna in a coating of fresh herbs and spices brings a new dimension to a classic French recipe. Crisp romaine lettuce leaves are tossed with a colorful array of chilled tomatoes, green beans, and pungent, briny kalamata olives. Garnished with hard-boiled eggs, red onions, and new potatoes, this Salade Niçoise is the perfect summer meal to enjoy on a shady patio.

NIÇOISE VINAIGRETTE:
> ¹/₂ cup balsamic vinegar
> ¹/₄ cup canned low-sodium chicken broth
> 2 tablespoons anchovy paste or finely chopped anchovy fillets
> 2 tablespoons roughly chopped capers
> ¹/₄ cup pitted, finely chopped kalamata olives
> 1 teaspoon minced fresh thyme leaves
> ¹/₄ cup extra-virgin olive oil
> Pinch of white pepper
> Sea salt

SALAD:
> 8 small red new potatoes, unpeeled
> 1 teaspoon salt
> 3 cups haricots verts or tender green beans, trimmed
> 1 head romaine lettuce, washed, dried, cut crosswise into 1-inch pieces, and chilled
> 1 medium red tomato, cored, seeded, and cut into thin wedges
> 1 medium yellow tomato, cored, seeded, and cut into thin wedges
> 1 cup kalamata olives, pitted and thinly sliced
> Freshly ground black pepper
> ¹/₃ cup finely diced red onion
> 1 tablespoon snipped chives
> 4 hard-boiled eggs, quartered

TUNA:
> 4 (5- to 6-ounce) ahi or albacore tuna steaks, without skin
> 2¹/₂ teaspoons extra-virgin olive oil
> 1 tablespoon chopped parsley
> 1 teaspoon fresh thyme leaves
> ¹/₄ teaspoon garlic salt
> Freshly ground black pepper

To prepare the vinaigrette: In a small bowl, combine all the vinaigrette ingredients except the olive oil, white pepper, and salt. Whisking continuously, slowly drizzle the oil into the mixture until the vinaigrette attains a thick and homogeneous consistency. Season with white pepper and, if needed, sea salt. Refrigerate for later use.

Put the potatoes in a large pot, add water to cover plus $1/2$ teaspoon of the salt, and simmer until a knife pierces the potatoes easily, about 25 minutes. Drain and allow to cool. Cut into $1/4$-inch slices and set aside.

Prepare an ice bath by filling a large bowl or pan with ice and cold water. Bring $1\ 1/2$ quarts of water to a boil and add the remaining $1/2$ teaspoon of salt. Cook the haricots verts until they are crisp-tender yet still vibrantly green, about 4 minutes. Drain and immediately plunge the beans into the ice bath to stop their cooking and preserve their bright green color. Drain and keep chilled in the refrigerator, covered with a damp towel.

Preheat a barbecue grill. Place the tuna steaks in a single layer on a plate or baking sheet. In a small cup, combine the olive oil, parsley, thyme, garlic salt, and pepper. Mix well. Rub the herb paste on both sides of each tuna steak. Close to serving time, place the tuna on the grill and sear each side, 3 to 4 minutes per side. The outside of the tuna should have charred grill marks and the center should be slightly pink. If you overcook this fish, it will be too firm and dry. (Alternatively, preheat the oven broiler with the shelf positioned closest to the heat. An oven broiler will work just fine, although the finished product will lack the grill marks and charred crispness.) Slice each tuna steak into 4 long, thin pieces.

To serve the salad, toss the lettuce, tomatoes, green beans, and olives with about half of the vinaigrette until well coated. Taste and add more vinaigrette as needed, and season with a grinding of black pepper.

Mound equal amounts of the dressed salad in the center of each plate. Arrange sliced potatoes around the tossed greens, drizzle some of the remaining vinaigrette over the ring of potatoes, and sprinkle with red onion and chives. Lean 4 strips of each grilled tuna steak up against each of the salad mounds. Place the wedges of hard-boiled eggs around the edge of each plate as garnish. Pass any remaining dressing separately at the table.

VARIATIONS AND SUGGESTIONS:

For an extra zing, add some Dijon mustard to the vinaigrette. Or, in addition to the balsamic vinegar, for a change of taste, you can also add some freshly squeezed lemon juice and Champagne vinegar.

NUTRITIONAL ANALYSIS PER SERVING:
Calories: 662 • Protein: 47.1 grams • Carbohydrates: 43.8 grams • Fiber: 8.12 grams • Fat: Total: 34 grams • Saturated: 6.45 grams • Cholesterol: 267 milligrams • Sodium: 750 milligrams

Slim Greek Tuna Salad

Serves 4

any times when Cher is stringently watching her fat intake on the advice of a doctor or nutritionist, I devise meals emphasizing the addition of flavorful ingredients while reducing the fat. This salad is one example. Here, tuna is combined with assertive ingredients like roasted bell pepper, kalamata olives, mustard, and fresh herbs—a refreshingly low-fat way to jazz it up.

2 cans (12 ounces each) solid white tuna in water, drained
1½ tablespoons Dijon mustard, or more
Juice of 1 lemon
1 teaspoon extra-virgin olive oil
1 teaspoon crushed dried oregano
½ teaspoon freshly ground black pepper
¼ teaspoon garlic salt
Pinch of sea salt
Pinch of celery salt
1½ cups diced hothouse cucumber
1 large roasted red bell pepper (see page 37), diced
¼ cup sliced pitted kalamata olives
¼ cup chopped parsley
1 tablespoon snipped fresh dill

In a mixing bowl, break up the tuna with a large spoon until it crumbles into fine pieces. Add and thoroughly incorporate the mustard, lemon juice, and olive oil. Mix in the oregano, pepper, garlic salt, sea salt, and celery salt. Add the cucumber, roasted bell pepper, olives, parsley, and dill. Gently mix until thoroughly combined. Taste and, if desired, season with additional Dijon mustard, salt, or black pepper. Serve chilled.

VARIATIONS AND SUGGESTIONS:
Try serving this salad in a cored and semiquartered whole tomato, on top of a bed of chilled salad greens, or as a sandwich on an herbed focaccia or dill bread.

NUTRITIONAL ANALYSIS PER SERVING:
Calories: 268 • Protein: 51.6 grams • Carbohydrates: 5.35 grams • Fiber: 1.34 grams • Fat: Total: 3.56 grams • Saturated: 0.615 gram • Cholesterol: 30.6 milligrams • Sodium: 369 milligrams

HOW TO PEEL AND SEED FRESH TOMATOES

Bring water to a boil in a small saucepan. Meanwhile, remove the stems from the tomatoes. On the reverse end, slice an X through the skin. Place the tomatoes in the boiling water for about 1 minute, or until the skin begins to loosen or crack. Remove the tomatoes with a slotted spoon and immerse them in a bowl of ice water or hold under cold running water. Once they cool, peel the skin off with a paring knife.

To remove the seeds, cut the tomatoes crosswise into halves and gently squeeze out the seeds. Use your finger if you have to in order to extract all the seeds. Cut the remaining tomato flesh into the size called for in your specific recipe.

Cher's Tuna Pasta Salad

Makes 9 cups; serves 4 to 6

This is one of Cher's old family favorites that I just couldn't resist including here. It makes me think of the sixties and seventies: tuna noodle casseroles, tie-dye, and Cher singing "Bell Bottom Blues." It began as a rich dish, high in fat, but Cher loved it so much that I created an updated lower-fat version that would fit into her diet. This salad has become a tradition at Cher's summer picnics and barbecues, and it is perfect for large groups —just multiply all the ingredients by whatever factor you desire.

> 1/2 pound pasta shells or gnocchi-shaped pasta
> 1 can (12 ounces) solid white tuna in water, drained
> 1/4 cup light or fat-free mayonnaise
> 2 medium tomatoes, peeled, seeded, and chopped (2 cups) (see page 77)
> 3/4 cup chopped celery
> 1 can (2 1/4 ounces) sliced black olives, drained
> 3 tablespoons finely chopped parsley
> 2 tablespoons finely snipped fresh dill, plus extra for garnish
> 1/2 teaspoon Beau Monde seasoning, or more
> Salt
> Freshly ground black pepper

Bring 3 quarts of salted water to a boil. Cook the pasta until al dente and drain in a colander. Rinse the pasta with cold running water until cool.

In a large mixing bowl, break up the tuna with a large spoon until it crumbles into fine pieces. Thoroughly incorporate the mayonnaise. Gently mix in the tomatoes, celery, olives, parsley, dill, and Beau Monde seasoning.

Add the pasta and lightly mix all the ingredients until evenly combined. Season with salt, pepper, and additional Beau Monde, as desired. Serve chilled. Garnish with a sprinkling of snipped fresh dill.

VARIATIONS AND SUGGESTIONS:

For a beautiful presentation, try this salad stuffed in steamed and chilled artichokes. Serve some of Cher's Ranch Dressing (page 31) on the side for dipping the artichoke leaves.

NUTRITIONAL ANALYSIS PER SERVING (2 1/4-cup serving):
Calories: 395 • Protein: 29.9 grams • Carbohydrates: 48.2 grams • Fiber: 2.94 grams • Fat: Total: 8.56 grams • Saturated: 1.59 grams • Cholesterol: 25.5 milligrams • Sodium: 568 milligrams

Seafood

Sole Meunière   81

Grilled Tuna and Papaya-Mint Salsa   82

Salmon en Papillote   83

Cajun Swordfish Brochettes   85

Crisp Sea Scallops in Spicy Roasted
Red Pepper Sauce   87

Fiery Pepper Shrimp Fried Rice   89

Shrimp Borracho   91

Sole Meunière

Serves 6

A very quick preparation for an elegant meal when you are short on time. Meunière, a French culinary word, refers to this style of cooking, in which thin sole fillets are dredged in seasoned flour and simply pan-fried. The addition of piquant capers, chopped parsley, and lemon juice adds pungent flavors to this mild, tender fish.

SEASONED FLOUR:
   1/2 cup flour
   1/4 teaspoon salt
   1/4 teaspoon freshly ground black pepper
SOLE:
   6 petrale sole fillets (about 1 1/2 pounds), rinsed and patted dry
   4 teaspoons Dijon mustard, or more, to taste
   2 teaspoons butter, or vegetable oil cooking spray
   3 tablespoons capers
   1 lemon, halved
   2 to 3 tablespoons chopped parsley

In a small bowl, mix together the flour, salt, and pepper.

Remove any bones from the sole, using tweezers or pliers if necessary. Coat each sole fillet with the mustard. In two large nonstick skillets over medium heat, melt the butter until bubbly but not browned. Dredge the sole fillets in the seasoned flour and place in a single layer in the skillets.

Cook the fish about 3 minutes on the first side, until the fillets begin to brown lightly. Gently turn them, using a long spatula. Over each fillet, sprinkle capers, a liberal squeeze of fresh lemon juice, and some of the chopped parsley. Cook until the fish is opaque all the way through, about 3 to 4 minutes on the second side. Serve at once, garnished with the rest of the parsley.

NUTRITIONAL ANALYSIS PER SERVING:
Calories: 160 • Protein: 23 grams • Carbohydrates: 9.3 grams • Fiber: 1 gram • Fat: Total: 3 grams • Saturated: 1 gram • Cholesterol: 9.3 milligrams • Sodium: 436 milligrams

Grilled Tuna and Papaya-Mint Salsa

Serves 4

*A*erb-rubbed tuna, fresh from the grill, is perfectly com-
plemented by this fruity salsa, a sweet-hot condiment
that can accompany any grilled seafood, crisp-roasted
chicken, or even heavy-flavor game meats like duck. The salsa is better if allowed to
macerate for 20 minutes or more.

Papaya-Mint Salsa:
  2½ cups diced peeled, seeded fresh papaya (about 2)
  ¼ cup finely diced red onion
  2 teaspoons minced seeded jalapeño
  1 tablespoon chopped fresh mint
  2 tablespoons distilled white vinegar or white wine vinegar
  Dash of sea salt

Grilled Tuna:
  4 ahi or albacore tuna steaks, without skin (each 6 ounces, cut ¾ inch
    thick)
  2 teaspoons extra-virgin olive oil
  2 to 3 tablespoons finely chopped mixed fresh herbs: lemon thyme,
    thyme, chives, tarragon, or a little rosemary
  1 tablespoon chopped parsley
  ¼ teaspoon garlic salt, or more
  Freshly ground black pepper

To prepare the salsa: Combine the papaya, red onion, jalapeño, mint, vinegar, and
salt in a small, nonmetallic bowl. Stir well. Cover and refrigerate until needed.

Preheat a barbecue grill. (Alternatively, preheat the oven broiler with the shelf
positioned closest to the heat. An oven broiler will work just fine, although the
finished product will lack the grill marks and the charred crispness.) Arrange
the tuna steaks in a single layer on a plate or baking sheet.

Combine the oil, herbs, parsley, garlic salt, and pepper. Mix well. Rub the
herb paste onto both sides of the tuna steaks. Grill the steaks for 3 to 4 minutes
on each side. The outside of the tuna should have charred grill marks and the
center should be slightly pink. (Tuna is best cooked no more than this; otherwise
it becomes too firm and dry.) Spoon the salsa over the tuna steaks and serve.

Nutritional Analysis per Serving:
Calories: 305 • Protein: 40.3 grams • Carbohydrates: 10.00 grams • Fiber: 1.82 grams • Fat: Total:
10.7 grams • Saturated: 2.49 grams • Cholesterol: 64.6 milligrams • Sodium: 155 milligrams

Salmon en Papillote

Serves 4

*B*aking fish, such as salmon, (or many other foods) in baking parchment is an excellent, fat-free method of cooking. This salmon lies on a bed of colorful julienned vegetables, sprinkled with white wine, and is completely enclosed in its own parchment pouch. As it bakes, the fish steams from the vegetable and wine juices, so that when the pouch is cut open, a wonderful fragrant steam is released and the moist fish is ready to eat. I often prepare this for dinner parties because it can all be assembled ahead of time, then baked at the last minute. Excellent accompaniments are Chastity's Italian Spinach and Onions (page 153) or Chilled Asparagus with Balsamic Vinaigrette (page 33), and a wild rice pilaf.

2 medium carrots, cut into julienne pieces 3 to 4 inches long
2 large stalks celery, cut into julienne pieces 3 to 4 inches long
2 to 3 teaspoons Dijon mustard
4 salmon fillets (7 to 8 ounces each), skin removed
1/4 to 1/2 teaspoon garlic salt
Freshly ground black pepper
1 lemon, peeled and cut into segments
2 to 3 tablespoons white wine
4 fresh dill sprigs, for garnish

In a pot fitted with a steamer insert, bring an inch or two of water to a boil and steam the carrots and celery, covered, until crisp-tender, 2 to 3 minutes. Remove the steamer insert and allow the vegetables to cool. Toss to thoroughly mix the vegetables.

Lay out four 12 x 15-inch sheets baking parchment on a flat, dry surface. Fold each in half widthwise, then reopen. Place an equal amount of the carrot-celery mixture in the middle of one of the halves of each parchment sheet.

Spread mustard over the top of each salmon fillet. Lightly sprinkle each fillet with garlic salt and pepper. Place a fillet on top of each bed of vegetables. Divide the lemon segments among the fillets. Sprinkle each portion with some of the wine.

Fold the empty half of each piece of parchment over the salmon. Starting at one corner of the parchment, where the fold was originally made, begin making short, overlapping folds to close up the open sides. Tightly crease each fold until you have reached the other end. At this point the packet should look like a crescent. Twist the loose end or use a paper clip to keep the paper from unfolding.

Place the pouches on a baking sheet. (The salmon can be prepared, assembled, and refrigerated to this point up to 3 hours in advance of cooking.)

About 15 minutes before baking, preheat the oven to 350 degrees F.

Place the salmon packets in the preheated oven and bake 15 to 18 minutes. Check for doneness by cutting open one of the pouches, being careful not to burn yourself from the steam that will be released. Using a knife, cut open the thickest part of the salmon fillet and check to see that it is cooked through and flaking.

Serve the salmon either en papillote, letting the diners cut away and discard the paper at the table, or remove the paper in advance and serve the fish with its embellishments on heated plates. In any case, garnish each fillet with a sprig of fresh dill.

NUTRITIONAL ANALYSIS PER SERVING:
Calories: 316 • Protein: 40.2 grams • Carbohydrates: 6.16 grams • Fiber: 1.68 grams • Fat: Total: 13 grams • Saturated: 1.98 grams • Cholesterol: 109 milligrams • Sodium: 330 milligrams

Cajun Swordfish Brochettes

Makes six 10-inch brochettes, serves 6

Succulent pieces of swordfish and colorful vegetables are coated with Cajun blackening spices, threaded onto skewers, and grilled or broiled until slightly charred. The combination of sweet, charred vegetables and hot Cajun spices make this low-fat preparation very tasty. Serve the swordfish brochettes with the Black-Eyed Pea Salad (page 43) or on a bed of Lemon-Dill Rice (page 172).

1 medium red onion, peeled and cut into 6 wedges
$^1/_2$ medium yellow or green bell pepper, cut into 1$^1/_4$-inch squares
    (6 pieces)
$^1/_2$ medium red bell pepper, cut into 1$^1/_4$-inch squares (6 pieces)
1 medium leek, tough green leaves removed, white stem cut crosswise
    into 1$^1/_4$-inch-long sections, washed thoroughly (6 pieces)
2 pounds skinless swordfish steaks (1$^1/_4$ to 1$^1/_2$ inches thick), cut into
    1$^1/_4$- to 1$^1/_2$-inch cubes (18 pieces)
1 tablespoon plus 2 teaspoons Cajun spice blend (see page 23)
2 teaspoons extra-virgin olive oil
2 tablespoons chopped parsley
6 whole white mushrooms, scrubbed and rinsed
6 (10-inch) bamboo skewers, soaked in water, or metal skewers

Preheat a barbecue grill to medium hot. (Alternatively, preheat the oven broiler with a shelf positioned closest to the heat.)

Place the red onion, bell peppers, and leek on a microwavable dish. Loosely cover with microwave-safe plastic wrap. Microwave the vegetables on High (100% power) for 4 to 5 minutes to soften. Remove the plastic wrap and set aside to cool. (Alternatively, steam the vegetables in a covered pot fitted with a steamer insert until softened, 4 to 5 minutes. Remove the steamer insert and allow the vegetables to cool.)

Lay the swordfish pieces on a plate. Sprinkle 1 tablespoon plus 1 teaspoon of the Cajun spice blend on all sides of the swordfish.

Combine the olive oil, parsley, and remaining 1 teaspoon Cajun spice blend in a large bowl. Add the microwaved vegetables and the mushrooms. Toss gently to coat.

On each skewer, thread the ingredients in this order: red onion, swordfish cube, yellow bell pepper, swordfish, leek, swordfish, red bell pepper, mushroom cap.

Using long-handled tongs, place the brochettes on the grill and cook until lightly blackened, about 5 minutes. Turn and continue to grill a few more minutes until the swordfish is cooked through and flakes easily with a fork. (Alternatively, place the brochettes on a baking sheet and broil, following the same instructions as for the grilling method.) Serve.

VARIATIONS AND SUGGESTIONS:

Feel free to use other vegetables; many times in the summer, when fresh corn is in season, I substitute corn on the cob in place of the leeks. Shuck one ear of corn, cut the cob in half lengthwise, and divide the halves into 2-inch sections. Toss with Cajun spice blend and other ingredients as directed. To attach the corn, forcefully push the skewer through the cob (a metal skewer makes this much easier). Always push the skewer downward through the cob onto a work surface. This will eliminate any possibility of stabbing yourself with the skewer.

NUTRITIONAL ANALYSIS PER SERVING (one skewer):
Calories: 205 • Protein: 30.8 grams • Carbohydrates: 6.15 grams • Fiber: 1.17 grams • Fat: Total: 7.8 grams • Saturated: 1.89 grams • Cholesterol: 58.9 milligrams • Sodium: 536 milligrams

Crisp Sea Scallops in Spicy Roasted Red Pepper Sauce

Serves 6

ven if seafood isn't your favorite dish, you will love this. It gives people the illusion of eating something deep-fried, though it is actually baked. I serve this to Cher as a ring of scallops on top of a red bell pepper sauce, like jewels on a red necklace.

For a different and more substantial presentation, serve a tossed salad of mixed baby greens with Balsamic Vinaigrette (page 33), or the Black-Eyed Pea Salad (page 43) in the center of each plate, surrounded by the sauce and crispy scallops. This makes a beautiful summer lunch or light dinner.

SCALLOPS:
  2 pounds large sea scallops (about 30)
  2 tablespoons Dijon mustard
  2$1/2$ teaspoons minced garlic
  $1/2$ cup flour, seasoned with salt and pepper
  4 egg whites, beaten
  1$1/2$ cups yellow cornmeal
  3 tablespoons minced parsley
  Vegetable oil cooking spray
ROASTED RED PEPPER SAUCE:
  3 large shallots, roughly chopped (about $1/4$ cup)
  1 stalk celery, sliced (about $1/2$ cup)
  1 cup vegetable broth, or more
  2 roasted red bell peppers (see page 37), roughly chopped
  1 bay leaf
  1 sprig fresh thyme
  $1/2$ teaspoon cayenne

  2 ears fresh corn, shucked, for garnish

Rinse the scallops in cold water, drain well, and pat dry. Place them in a bowl and toss gently with the Dijon mustard and minced garlic. Set aside. Use three small bowls for dredging the scallops, placing the seasoned flour in one, the egg whites in another, and the cornmeal and parsley combined in the third.

To prepare the sauce: In a medium saucepan over low heat, combine the shallots, celery, and 2 tablespoons of the vegetable broth. Cover the pot and allow the vegetables to sweat lightly (see page 60) for about 5 minutes, until softened. Uncover the saucepan and add the remaining vegetable broth, the chopped bell peppers, the bay leaf, thyme, and cayenne. Bring to a gentle boil, reduce the heat, and simmer, covered, about 15 minutes.

Preheat the oven to 400 degrees F., with a shelf positioned in the upper third of the oven.

Take the red pepper mixture off the heat. Remove and discard the bay leaf and thyme sprig. Purée the remaining mixture in a blender or food processor fitted with a metal blade. The sauce should have a consistency thick enough to coat the back of a spoon. If it is too thick, thin it with additional vegetable broth. Keep warm.

Meanwhile, roast the corn in the preheated oven, turning several times, until the kernels are a darkish brown, 10 to 15 minutes. Remove from the oven. When the corn is cool enough to handle, cut the kernels from the ears and set aside in a small bowl. (The scallops, red pepper sauce, and corn can be prepared to this point 2 hours in advance.)

Coat a baking sheet with a thin film of cooking spray. Arrange the three bowls of dredging ingredients and the scallops on your counter. One at a time, dredge the scallops in the seasoned flour, then in the egg whites, then in the cornmeal mixture. (It helps to use one hand for dipping in the dry ingredients and the other for the egg whites, so that the ingredients do not stick so much to your hands.) Place the coated scallops on the prepared baking sheet and, when finished, spray additional cooking spray over their tops.

Bake the scallops until golden brown and firm, about 10 minutes. (Alternatively, the scallops can be sautéed in a large skillet over medium-high heat.)

To serve, spoon the red pepper sauce around the center of each dinner plate. Arrange 5 scallops in a ring on the sauce on each plate, and garnish with a scattering of the roasted corn kernels.

NUTRITIONAL ANALYSIS PER SERVING:
Calories: 335 • Protein: 33.2 grams • Carbohydrates: 44.5 grams • Fiber: 4.72 grams • Fat: Total: 2.74 grams • Saturated: 0.284 grams • Cholesterol: 49.9 milligrams • Sodium: 710 milligrams

Fiery Pepper Shrimp Fried Rice

Makes 9 cups; serves 6

If this came in a bottle, I think it would have little red devils dancing over fire on the label. I developed this recipe for Cher because she loves pepper, spicy food, and shrimp fried rice, so I combined all of these for a marriage made in . . . well, you get the idea. This recipe offers many varied contrasts that tease your senses and lead one into temptation: crispy shrimp, blistering hot spices, and soft, mellowing rice. Can you resist?

All of this can be achieved by sautéing the shrimp over high heat in one pan and "frying" the rice in another. Be sure to do this in a well-ventilated kitchen so you do not inadvertently breathe in the hot pepper fumes.

1/4 teaspoon dark sesame oil
1 tablespoon peanut oil or vegetable oil
1 large onion, diced
3 medium carrots, cut into short julienne pieces
1/2 to 3/4 cup julienned red bell pepper
13/4 cups raw brown rice, prepared according to package directions and
    kept warm
2 teaspoons or more low-sodium soy sauce
3 green onions, thinly sliced, plus extra for garnish
1/2 cup frozen green peas, thawed
11/2 pounds medium shrimp, peeled, deveined, rinsed, and patted dry
1/2 to 3/4 teaspoon cayenne
3/4 teaspoon freshly ground black pepper
1/2 teaspoon garlic salt
2 tablespoons toasted slivered almonds (optional)

In a large sauté pan or wok, heat the sesame oil and 1 teaspoon of the peanut oil over medium-high heat. Add the onion, carrots, and red bell peppers and lightly brown about 6 to 8 minutes. Stir in the cooked rice and continue cooking another 2 to 3 minutes. Add the soy sauce. Stir well. Mix in the green onions and peas. Pour the mixture into a bowl and keep warm. Rinse and dry the pan.

In a bowl, evenly coat the shrimp with the cayenne, black pepper, and garlic salt.

In the sauté pan, heat the remaining 2 teaspoons of peanut oil over high heat. When it is very hot and wisps of smoke appear, add the shrimp and allow them to brown and crisp on one side before shaking the pan to turn them. (During this step, be careful not to breathe the smoke coming off the cooking shrimp. The smoking spices can be very irritating.) The shrimp will be fully cooked in 4 to 5 minutes. Add the shrimp to the bowl of fried rice and vegetables. Add the toasted almonds, if using, and mix thoroughly. Serve hot, garnished with a sprinkling of sliced green onions.

NUTRITIONAL ANALYSIS PER SERVING:
Calories: 375 • Protein: 29.7 grams • Carbohydrates: 50.6 grams • Fiber: 4.26 grams • Fat: Total: 5.43 grams • Saturated: 1.07 grams • Cholesterol: 221 milligrams • Sodium: 429 milligrams

Shrimp Borracho

Serves 4 as an entrée, 8 as an appetizer

Shrimp borracho, or camarones borracho, *means "drunken shrimp"* *in Spanish. The Tex-Mex appeal of this dish comes from the liberal* *use of garlic, cilantro, and tomatillos (a Mexican green tomato-like* *fruit with a dry husk), with a hint of lime and smoky tequila. These saucy shrimp* *may be served as an appetizer with warmed corn tortillas, or as a more substantial* *entrée with Fat-free Black Beans (page 175) and Vibrant Verde Rice (page 171).*

Thanks go to my mentor and friend, Christian Chavanne, who developed this *dish and with whom I served countless spa guests while I was cooking at the Four* *Seasons Resort in Dallas, Texas.*

2 teaspoons butter
4 green onions, thinly sliced
1/3 cup minced garlic
1 1/4 pounds plum tomatoes, peeled, seeded, and diced
1 1/4 pounds (about 14 to 16 medium) tomatillos, husks removed, rinsed and diced, or 1 can (28 ounces) tomatillos, drained and diced
1 1/2 teaspoons dried thyme
1 1/2 teaspoons crushed dried Mexican oregano
Pinch of cayenne
1 teaspoon all-purpose seasoning, such as Spike or Veg-it
1/3 cup coarsely chopped cilantro (or parsley), plus extra for garnish
1 1/2 pounds large shrimp, peeled and deveined (16 to 18 shrimp)
1/3 cup fresh lime juice
2 tablespoons tequila
Garlic salt
Freshly ground black pepper

Melt the butter in a large skillet over medium-high heat. Sauté the green onions and garlic about 1 minute without browning. Add the tomatoes, tomatillos, thyme, oregano, cayenne, all-purpose seasoning, and cilantro. Cook about 5 minutes, or until the tomato mixture is softened and juicy.

Add the shrimp, cover the skillet, and cook about 3 minutes, until the shrimp begin to turn pink. Stir in the lime juice and tequila and continue to cook, covered, another 4 to 5 minutes. Remove lid and adjust the seasoning, if necessary, with garlic salt and black pepper.

Neatly arrange the shrimp on plates with the accumulated sauce spooned over them.

NUTRITIONAL ANALYSIS PER SERVING (based on 4 large shrimp per serving):
Calories: 303 • Protein: 39.1 grams • Carbohydrates: 21 grams • Fiber: 4.7 grams • Fat: Total: 5.8 grams • Saturated: 1.77 grams • Cholesterol: 336 milligrams • Sodium: 579 milligrams

Poultry

Olive Tapenade Chicken

Serves 8

his is a signature dish that I developed and served while working under Chef Lydia Shire at the Four Seasons Hotel in Beverly Hills. It has since become one of my most popular and coveted recipes. Cher calls this dish "Chicken from Hell" because the taste is so amazingly delicious it's almost sinful!

Olive tapenade is a puréed paste of oil-cured black olives, garlic, and capers, with a boldly assertive flavor. Chicken breasts are enrobed in this tapenade, then blanketed in fresh bread crumbs and baked until crispy. They are the ideal accompaniment to Rustic Grilled Tomato Sauce and Pasta (page 95). The combination of flavors and aromas from the heady olives and the sweet, smoky tomato sauce is a marriage made in heaven. Serve asparagus or Cut Grilled Vegetables (page 156) on the side.

OLIVE TAPENADE:
- 4½ ounces (¾ cup) oil-cured black olives
- 1 tablespoon plus 1 teaspoon capers
- 2¼ teaspoons chopped garlic
- 2 teaspoons chopped anchovy fillets
- 1 tablespoon plus 2 teaspoons fresh lemon juice
- 1 teaspoon white wine
- 2 tablespoons extra-virgin olive oil
- Vegetable oil cooking spray

BREADING:
- 2 cups medium-coarse fresh sourdough bread crumbs
- ¼ cup finely chopped parsley
- ¼ teaspoon freshly ground black pepper

- 8 boneless, skinless chicken breast halves (about 2½ pounds), rinsed and patted dry

To prepare the tapenade: Pit the olives by squeezing each olive between your thumb and forefinger until the olive splits and the pit can be removed. In a food processor fitted with a metal blade, or in a blender, combine the olives, capers, garlic, anchovies, lemon juice, and wine. Process until coarsely chopped. With the motor running, slowly add a steady stream of the olive oil to make a smooth, thick paste. Set aside in a small bowl.

Preheat the oven to 425 degrees F. Coat a baking sheet with a thin film of vegetable oil cooking spray.

Combine the fresh bread crumbs, parsley, and pepper in a shallow bowl.

Rub all sides of each chicken breast with the olive paste until well covered. Roll each chicken breast in the bread crumbs, pressing on the crumbs to adhere. Place the chicken breasts on the baking sheet. Bake until firm and golden brown, 10 to 12 minutes. (If the breasts are not completely browned and crisp, broil them about 2 minutes, watching carefully so the breading does not burn.)

To serve, slice each cooked breast at an angle, crosswise, into 4 to 5 strips and fan out on plates.

NUTRITIONAL ANALYSIS PER SERVING:
Calories: 357 • Protein: 31.2 grams • Carbohydrates: 22.3 grams • Fiber: 2.39 grams • Fat: Total: 13.2 grams • Saturated: 1.78 grams • Cholesterol: 70 milligrams • Sodium: 791 milligrams

Chicken Sausage Lasagna

Serves 10 as an entrée for a sit-down dinner;
12 at a buffet dinner

he hallmark of this lasagna recipe is the Bolognese-style sauce, which usually contains high-fat Italian sausage or beef. I have used ground chicken with a blend of "sausage" herbs and spices, which results in a sauce so low in fat and so delicious you could eat it in a bowl on its own. Although the preparation is time-consuming, this is a perfect make-ahead dish, and one well worth the effort. It makes an ample amount and is a perfect party dish. It freezes beautifully, so you could bake half now and freeze half for later, if you wished, simply by preparing it in two smaller (8 x 8 x 2-inch) baking dishes.

3 medium eggplants (about 3 pounds), peeled and cut lengthwise into 1/4-inch-thick slices
1 tablespoon salt

CHICKEN SAUSAGE:
2 pounds ground chicken
1 teaspoon minced garlic
2 teaspoons fennel seed
2 teaspoons paprika
1 teaspoon kosher salt or regular salt
2 teaspoons dried rubbed sage
1/2 teaspoon dried thyme
1/2 teaspoon Italian herb seasoning
1/2 teaspoon crushed red pepper
1 teaspoon crushed dried oregano
2 teaspoons crushed dried basil
1 teaspoon onion powder

CHICKEN SAUSAGE BOLOGNESE SAUCE:
2 tablespoons extra-virgin olive oil
5 cups chopped onions
3 tablespoons minced garlic
1 recipe chicken sausage mixture (above)
1/4 teaspoon cayenne
1/4 teaspoon black pepper
3 or 4 bay leaves
1 tablespoon crushed dried basil
1 teaspoon crushed dried oregano
1/2 teaspoon celery seed
1 teaspoon salt

1 can (28 ounces) tomato purée
2 cans (28 ounces each) Italian-style whole tomatoes with liquid, the
    tomatoes coarsely chopped
3 cups peeled and chopped fresh plum tomatoes
1 tablespoon sugar
ASSEMBLY INGREDIENTS:
    Olive oil cooking spray
    Reserved salted eggplant slices (above)
    Garlic salt blend, to taste
    Freshly ground black pepper, to taste
    3 containers (8 ounces each) fat-free ricotta cheese
    1 extra-large whole egg
    $^1/_3$ cup chopped parsley
    10 curly-edged lasagna noodles
    $^1/_3$ cup grated fat-free mozzarella (optional)

Place the eggplant slices in 2 quarts of lukewarm water with the salt added. This leaches any bitterness out of the eggplant. Set aside to soak.

Thoroughly mix together all the chicken sausage ingredients in a medium bowl. Reserve.

To prepare the sauce: Heat the olive oil in a large, wide pot over medium heat. Sauté the onions and garlic until soft, about 10 minutes. Add the reserved chicken sausage mixture in small pieces. Cook until the sausage mixture begins to turn opaque, breaking up any clumps with a wooden spoon. Add the cayenne, black pepper, bay leaves, basil, oregano, celery seed, and salt. Stir well and continue to cook 3 to 4 minutes. Add all of the tomato products and the sugar. Bring the sauce to a simmer and cook for 1 hour, stirring occasionally.

Meanwhile, preheat the oven to 350 degrees F. Bring a 6- to 8-quart pot of salted water to a boil.

To prepare the eggplant, spray a baking sheet with the olive oil cooking spray. Shake the excess water off the eggplant slices and place them on the sheet in a single layer (2 or 3 batches may be necessary). Sprinkle the garlic salt blend and pepper over the slices. Spray the tops of the slices with additional cooking spray to keep them moist while baking. Bake until soft, about 15 minutes. Sprinkle more water over the slices, if necessary, to prevent them from drying out and sticking to the sheet. Remove from the oven and set aside.

Combine the ricotta, egg, and parsley in a bowl. Set aside.

Boil the lasagna noodles in the salted water according to package directions, or until al dente. Drain and lay flat on damp kitchen towels.

Take the sauce off the heat and remove the bay leaves.

To assemble: In the bottom of a 4-quart 15 x 10 x 2-inch glass baking dish, spread 3 cups of the sauce. Cover with 5 lasagna noodles. Spread half the ricotta mixture over the pasta layer. Cover with half of the eggplant slices. Continue layering in this order: 3 cups of the sauce, remaining half of the eggplant slices, remaining ricotta mixture, 3 cups of the sauce, remaining lasagna noodles. Finish by topping with 3 cups of the sauce. If using, sprinkle the mozzarella over the top. Bake for 45 minutes until bubbling and heated through. (Place a tray under the lasagna to catch any sauce that may drip over.)

Remove the lasagna from the oven and allow it to set for at least 10 minutes to facilitate slicing. Using a serrated knife, divide the lasagna into 10 or 12 equal squares. Any additional sauce may be pooled on each plate or served on the side.

VARIATIONS AND SUGGESTIONS:
If you cannot find time to make the entire dish, prepare just the sauce and serve it over rigatoni, penne, or bow tie pasta.

NUTRITIONAL ANALYSIS PER SERVING (based on 12 servings):
Calories: 452 • Protein: 28 grams • Carbohydrates: 44.5 grams • Fiber: 8.2 grams • Fat: Total: 19.5 grams • Saturated: 9.7 grams • Cholesterol: 101 milligrams • Sodium: 1076 milligrams

Chicken Tamale Pie

Serves 6 to 8

*T*his crowd-pleasing dish shows off a bright-yellow cornmeal crust with a deep-red spicy chicken filling accented by Cher's favorite enchilada sauce. The great taste of this dish comes in part from using the broth in which the chicken is prepared to flavor the cornmeal crust. It's a wonderful dish for entertaining, since you can assemble it up to a day in advance and bake it when you're ready to serve.

CHICKEN:
    1 cup coarsely chopped or sliced celery
    $1/3$ cup coarsely chopped or sliced carrots
    $1^1/2$ cups coarsely chopped or sliced onion
    $1/3$ cup coarsely chopped cilantro, including stems
    2 teaspoons ground cumin
    1 teaspoon chili powder
    1 bay leaf, broken into pieces
    $1^1/2$ teaspoons salt
    3 or 4 chicken breast halves, on the bone (about $2^1/4$ pounds), rinsed
CHICKEN FILLING:
    1 tablespoon extra-virgin olive oil
    $1^3/4$ cups diced onion
    1 tablespoon minced garlic
    1 can ($14^1/2$ ounces) diced tomatoes and liquid
    1 teaspoon crushed dried Mexican oregano
    $1/2$ teaspoon dried thyme
    1 teaspoon ground cumin
    $1/2$ teaspoon chili powder
    1 can ($2^1/4$ ounces) sliced black olives, drained
    1 can (4 ounces) diced green chiles
    $3/4$ cup prepared red enchilada sauce (found in the Mexican food
        section of most grocery stores), plus extra for serving
    $1/4$ teaspoon salt (optional)
    Reserved shredded chicken (from above)
CORNMEAL CRUST:
    $1^1/3$ cups yellow cornmeal
    4 cups reserved chicken broth (from above)
    $1/4$ cup grated Cheddar cheese (optional)
    1 tablespoon chopped cilantro or parsley, for garnish

To prepare the chicken: In a medium bowl, combine the celery, carrots, onion, cilantro, cumin, chili powder, bay leaf, and salt. Mix to distribute everything evenly. Place half of this vegetable mixture in the bottom of a large, wide pot. Arrange the chicken breasts on top in a single layer. Cover the chicken with the remaining vegetable mixture. Add water to barely cover (about 4 to 5 cups). Cover the pot, bring to a gentle simmer, and cook until the chicken is firm, about 30 minutes.

Remove the chicken breasts and the vegetables from the broth and place them in a bowl until cool enough to handle. Strain the cooking mixture through a fine sieve and reserve the broth. (Enjoy the warm strained vegetables as a "cook's treat"; they are incredibly flavorful.) Rinse and dry the pot. Remove and discard the skin and bones from the chicken. Shred the chicken into fine strips and set aside.

To prepare the filling: In the clean pot, heat the olive oil over medium heat. Sauté the onion and garlic until soft, about 5 to 7 minutes. Add the tomatoes, oregano, thyme, cumin, chili powder, black olives, green chiles, enchilada sauce, and salt, if using. Stir well and cook, uncovered, about 10 minutes to allow the flavors to blend and the excess liquid to reduce. Stir in the reserved shredded chicken and set aside.

Preheat the oven to 350 degrees F.

To prepare the crust: In a small bowl, combine the cornmeal with 1 cup of the reserved chicken broth. In a medium saucepan, bring the remaining 3 cups of broth to a boil. Slowly add the wet cornmeal mixture to the boiling broth, whisking constantly. The mixture will thicken rapidly. Reduce the heat to low and cook, stirring constantly, for 3 to 4 minutes, then remove from the heat.

To assemble the tamale pie, spread half of the cornmeal mixture in the bottom of a 2-quart 8 x 11 x 2-inch glass baking dish. Place all of the chicken filling on top and cover with the remaining half of the cornmeal. (It's fine if some of the filling shows through in places.) Sprinkle with the cheese, if using. Bake for 25 to 30 minutes, until heated through. Garnish with the cilantro before serving. Pass additional warmed enchilada sauce on the side.

VARIATIONS AND SUGGESTIONS:

You can vary this recipe by substituting a tomatillo or green chile verde sauce for the red enchilada sauce.

NUTRITIONAL ANALYSIS PER SERVING:
Calories: 334 • Protein: 27.5 grams • Carbohydrates: 35.2 grams • Fiber: 4.72 grams • Fat: Total: 8.98 grams • Saturated: 3.77 grams • Cholesterol: 61.7 milligrams • Sodium: 842 milligrams

Chicken Enchiladas

Makes 12 enchiladas, 6 servings

Spicy shredded-chicken filling wrapped in corn tortillas and coated in a red chile enchilada sauce—a perfect Mexican meal with Grilled Corn and Green Chile Peppers (page 157), Vibrant Verde Rice (page 171), and Unfried Refried Beans (page 176). These enchiladas do take a little time to put together, but if you plan ahead, the chicken filling can be cooked a day in advance and the enchiladas assembled the next day. These enchiladas also freeze well and can be quickly heated in a microwave or conventional oven.

1 medium onion, peeled and sliced
1 medium carrot, peeled and sliced
1 stalk celery (with leaves), sliced
$1/3$ cup coarsely chopped cilantro, including stems
1 teaspoon ground cumin
$1/2$ teaspoon chili powder
1 teaspoon salt
8 black peppercorns, slightly crushed
3 chicken breast halves on the bone (about $2^{1/4}$ pounds), rinsed
1 can (19 ounces) prepared red enchilada sauce (found in the Mexican food section of most grocery stores)
Half of a $4^{1/4}$-ounce can chopped black olives
Half of a 4-ounce can diced green chiles
1 cup safflower oil or peanut oil
12 corn tortillas
$1/4$ cup grated Cheddar cheese (optional)
3 tablespoons chopped cilantro, for garnish

In a large bowl, combine the onion, carrot, celery, cilantro, cumin, chili powder, salt, and peppercorns. Toss to combine well. Place half of this aromatic mixture in the bottom of a medium-size pot. Arrange the chicken breasts on top in a single layer. Cover the chicken with the remaining vegetable mixture. Add water to barely cover (about 4 to 5 cups). Cover the pot, bring to a gentle simmer, and cook until the chicken is firm, about 30 minutes.

Remove the chicken from the broth and place it in a bowl until cool enough to handle. (Discard the cooking broth with the vegetables.) Remove and discard the skin and bones from the chicken. Shred the chicken into fine strips. In the bowl, combine the chicken with $2/3$ cup of the enchilada sauce, the black olives, and the green chiles. Mix well. Set aside. (The filling can be prepared up to 1 day ahead to this point and stored, covered and refrigerated, or frozen for up to 1 month.)

Set three large rimmed plates on your kitchen counter next to the stove: Cover one with several layers of paper towels, another with as much warmed enchilada sauce as it will hold, and leave empty the third. Have a 2-quart 8 x 11 x 2-inch glass baking dish ready.

In a small saucepan, heat the remaining enchilada sauce until it is barely simmering. In a medium skillet, carefully heat the oil over medium heat. The oil should be hot enough so that when a corn tortilla is dipped into it, small bubbles immediately rise to the surface. (Do not allow the oil to smoke, since it is then too hot and a fire could start. Also, be careful not to splash any other liquid into the oil, as it will splatter and could burn you.)

When the oil is ready to fry the corn tortillas, place one tortilla at a time in the oil, using long-handled tongs. Fry each tortilla until it begins to bulge and bubble, about 15 seconds. (Expect them to cook quickly.) Immediately turn the tortilla with the tongs and fry about 10 seconds more. Do not let it cook until it is crisp. Place the tortilla on the paper towels and blot off excess oil. Immediately dip it into the warmed enchilada sauce, and then put it on the empty plate. Spoon 1/4 cup of the chicken filling in a line across the tortilla and gently roll it up like a cigar. Place the filled tortilla, seam side down, in the glass baking dish. Repeat with the remaining tortillas, regulating the heat of the oil so it does not become too hot. When all of the tortillas have been fried, carefully remove the oil from the stove and let it cool before discarding.

Preheat the oven to 350 degrees F. shortly before you are ready to make the enchiladas.

Spoon a small amount of enchilada sauce over each of the filled tortillas. Cover with foil. (The enchiladas can be prepared up to 1 day ahead to this point and stored, covered and refrigerated, or frozen for quick meals anytime. Bring back to room temperature before baking.) Bake the enchiladas for 15 minutes, or until just heated through. (If you like, the grated Cheddar can be sprinkled over the enchiladas before they go in the oven.) Garnish with the chopped cilantro and serve the remaining enchilada sauce in a small pitcher or sauceboat.

NUTRITIONAL ANALYSIS PER SERVING (based on 6 servings per recipe):
Calories: 456 • Protein: 20 grams • Carbohydrates: 34 grams • Fiber: 4.5 grams • Fat: Total: 26.5 grams • Saturated: 8.53 grams • Cholesterol: 71 milligrams • Sodium: 375 milligrams

Turkey Chili

Serves 6 to 8

*B*old-flavored, yet incredibly low in fat, this chili is a household favorite. Everyone (including the chef) loves the fact that this can be heated at any time to make a great late-night nosh with pasta, tortillas, eggs, whatever. It can be prepared several days in advance and, as a matter of fact, the flavor improves. I devised the spice blend, which I believe to be an almost exact duplicate of a very famous "Texas-style" store-bought chili seasoning mix. Mexican Corn Bread (page 170) and Dill Coleslaw (page 42) are excellent accompaniments to put out the fire.

CHILI SPICE BLEND:
   1 tablespoon plus 1 teaspoon masa harina (available in the Mexican
      food section of the grocery store)
   3 tablespoons chili powder
   1 tablespoon plus 1 teaspoon ground cumin
   1 teaspoon paprika
   $1/4$ teaspoon cayenne
   $1/2$ teaspoon crushed dried Mexican oregano
   $1/2$ teaspoon salt
   $1/4$ teaspoon garlic salt
   $1/4$ teaspoon cocoa powder (optional)
TURKEY CHILI:
   1 tablespoon olive oil
   $4^{1}/_{2}$ to 5 cups diced onions
   1 tablespoon plus 2 teaspoons minced garlic
   $2^{1}/_{2}$ pounds ground turkey
   1 can (15 ounces) tomato sauce
   1 can (28 ounces) whole tomatoes and liquid, the tomatoes cut up
   1 can ($15^{1}/_{4}$ ounces) red kidney beans, drained and rinsed
   1 can (4 ounces) diced mild green chiles (optional)
GARNISHES:
   Grated low-fat Cheddar cheese
   Chopped red onion
   Chopped cilantro
   Low-fat or nonfat sour cream

Combine all of the chili spice blend ingredients in a small bowl and set aside.
   To prepare the chili: Heat the oil in a large wide pot over medium-high heat.

Sauté the onions and garlic until soft, about 10 minutes, stirring occasionally. Add the ground turkey and cook until it is opaque, about 7 to 8 minutes, breaking up any clumps with a wooden spoon while it cooks.

Add the spice blend and mix in thoroughly, continuing to cook for another 5 minutes.

Stir in the tomato sauce, tomatoes, kidney beans, and green chiles, if using. (You may want to add the chiles later, after tasting, to determine how spicy you want the chili.) Bring to a simmer and cook for about 45 minutes, or until thick, stirring occasionally to prevent sticking. Adjust seasoning to taste, adding more chili powder or green chiles if you want a spicier chili.

Serve the chili piping hot, garnished with the grated cheese, red onion, cilantro, and sour cream.

VARIATIONS AND SUGGESTIONS:
I have served this chili in many forms: with scrambled eggs and wrapped in flour tortillas, on top of penne pasta, or as a taco salad with the chili on top of shredded lettuce tossed with tortilla chips and all of the garnishes. Use your imagination!

NUTRITIONAL ANALYSIS PER SERVING (based on 6 servings per recipe and not including garnishes):
Calories: 479 • Protein: 46 grams • Carbohydrates: 24.4 grams • Fiber: 7.29 grams • Fat: Total: 21.9 grams • Saturated: 5.29 grams • Cholesterol: 146 milligrams • Sodium: 1280 milligrams

Chicken Satay and Thai Peanut Noodles

Serves 8

*T**his fabulous combination of crisp textures and spicy Thai flavors makes an exotic, festive dish to serve at a dinner party. I arrange the julienned vegetables in small, colorful bundles around the spicy noodles. Bamboo-skewered chicken adorns the noodles to make this a stunning display. For convenience, the peanut sauce, marinated chicken, and garnishes can be prepared up to 1 day in advance.*

16 to 20 (8-inch) bamboo or metal skewers

PEANUT SAUCE:
1/3 cup defatted natural-style peanut butter (pour off any accumulated oil floating on top)
1 tablespoon low-sodium soy sauce
2 tablespoons fresh lemon juice
1/2 teaspoon crushed red pepper
1 tablespoon chopped cilantro
2 tablespoons rice wine vinegar
1 teaspoon dark sesame oil
1 tablespoon minced garlic
1/2 cup plain nonfat yogurt

CHICKEN SATAY:
6 boneless, skinless chicken breasts halves (about 2 pounds), rinsed and patted dry
1/4 cup chopped cilantro
2 teaspoons low-sodium soy sauce

GARNISHES:
1 1/2 pounds asparagus, peeled, tough ends removed, stalks cut into 1 1/2-inch pieces
1/2 red bell pepper, cut into 1 1/2-inch julienne pieces
2 medium carrots, cut into 1 1/2-inch julienne pieces
1/2 hothouse cucumber, peeled, seeded, and cut into 1 1/2-inch julienne pieces
6 green onions, green parts included, thinly sliced on the diagonal
1/2 pound fresh bean sprouts

12 ounces dried udon noodles

In a food processor fitted with a metal blade, combine all of the peanut sauce ingredients and process until the sauce is smooth and homogeneous. Set aside.

To prepare the satay: Slice the chicken into 1/2-inch-wide strips. In a bowl, mix together 6 tablespoons of the peanut sauce, the cilantro, and the soy sauce. Add the chicken strips and marinate, covered and refrigerated, until ready to skewer and cook.

Preheat the oven to 450 degrees F. Soak the bamboo skewers in water so they do not burn when cooking.

To prepare the garnishes: Bring a shallow amount of water to a boil in a small pot fitted with a steamer insert. Place the asparagus in the steamer insert, cover, and steam 2 to 3 minutes until it is crisp-tender. Remove immediately and run cold running water over the asparagus to stop the cooking process and preserve the color. Drain and set aside in a bowl. Prepare the remaining garnishes and set aside in individual bowls.

Thread 1 or 2 strips of chicken onto each soaked bamboo skewer. Place them on a baking sheet and bake for 6 to 8 minutes, or until firm and cooked through.

Bring a 5-quart pot of water to a rolling boil. Plunge the noodles into the boiling water. Stirring them well, cook for about 6 to 7 minutes, or just until al dente. Drain thoroughly. Add the bean sprouts and the remaining peanut sauce and toss until the noodles are well coated.

Place individual noodle servings in wide shallow bowls (or use a large serving platter for a buffet presentation). Garnish by placing mounds of asparagus, red pepper, carrots, and cucumber around the noodles. Sprinkle the green onions over the noodles and place skewers of chicken satay on top.

VARIATIONS AND SUGGESTIONS:
This dish may be prepared cold as well, and is equally flavorful. Simply drain the cooked noodles and rinse with cold running water before tossing them with the bean sprouts and peanut sauce. The skewered chicken can be prepared and cooked in advance and allowed to cool, or cooked just prior to serving and placed on the cold noodles.

NUTRITIONAL ANALYSIS PER SERVING:
Calories: 362.50 • Protein: 32.03 grams • Carbohydrates: 42.55 grams • Fiber: 5.33 grams • Fat: Total: 8.05 grams • Saturated: 1.19 grams • Cholesterol: 51.6 milligrams • Sodium: 722 milligrams

Moroccan Chicken Stew and Couscous

Serves 8

her fell in love with this spicy, exotic dish, when I presented it as an "audition" for the job as her chef. She was preparing to move into a new home and I remember having to climb around boxes, exercise equipment, and assorted clutter as I put together what I hoped was just the right dish to impress her. The aromatic mix of coriander, cumin, cinnamon, and cloves brought a caravan of family and friends through the door, and the blend of spices and lively conversation reminded me more of being in a souk on market day than in a kitchen in Bel Air.

This dish was inspired by leading nutritional consultant and author Jeanne Jones, whom I had the wonderful opportunity to work with in developing the recipes for the Dallas Four Seasons Resort.

CHICKEN STEW:
    2 teaspoons extra-virgin olive oil
    2$^1/_2$ cups diced onions
    1 tablespoon minced garlic
    $^1/_4$ teaspoon whole saffron threads, or $^1/_8$ teaspoon powdered
    1$^3/_4$ pounds boneless, skinless chicken breast halves, cut into $^1/_2$-inch cubes
    2 teaspoons ground coriander
    1 teaspoon ground cumin
    $^1/_2$ teaspoon chili powder
    Pinch of ground cinnamon
    Pinch of ground cloves
    $^1/_2$ teaspoon salt
    1 can (14$^1/_2$ ounces) low-sodium chicken broth
    1 can (16 ounces) whole peeled tomatoes and liquid, the tomatoes quartered
    3 cups diced peeled turnips
    2$^1/_2$ cups diced peeled yams
    1 can (8$^3/_4$ ounces) garbanzo beans, drained and rinsed
    $^1/_4$ cup golden raisins
    1 tablespoon cornstarch mixed with 1 tablespoon water
COUSCOUS:
    $^1/_2$ teaspoon salt
    1 tablespoon butter (optional)

2 carrots, cut into julienne pieces, then cubed
$^{1}/_{4}$ cup chopped parsley, plus more for garnish
1 box (10 ounces) quick-cooking couscous (Moroccan pasta)

To prepare the stew: Heat the olive oil in a large wide pot over medium heat and sauté the onions and garlic until soft but not browned, about 6 minutes. Add the saffron and stir until well coated (the onions will turn a brilliant yellow). Add the chicken, coriander, cumin, chili powder, cinnamon, cloves, and salt, stirring to distribute the seasonings evenly. Add the chicken broth and simmer gently, covered, about 15 minutes.

Add the tomatoes, turnips, yams, garbanzo beans, and raisins. Stirring occasionally, simmer for another 25 minutes, until the vegetables are cooked through but not mushy. (If you do cook them to the mushy stage, don't worry; that is exactly the way Cher likes this! She loves the vegetables soft and falling apart.)

In a steady stream, while stirring, add the cornstarch and water mixture. Continue to simmer 2 to 3 minutes, until the stew has thickened. Remove from heat.

To prepare the couscous: In a medium pot, bring $2^{1}/_{4}$ cups of water, the salt, and butter, if using, to a boil. Add the carrots and $^{1}/_{4}$ cup of parsley and cook 1 minute. Pour the couscous into the boiling liquid, stir once, cover the pot, and immediately remove from the heat. Allow to stand 5 minutes, covered. Fluff the couscous with a fork.

Mound the couscous on plates or in individual soup bowls. Ladle the stew over each portion of couscous and garnish with chopped parsley.

NUTRITIONAL ANALYSIS PER SERVING:
Calories: 308 • Protein: 29.2 grams • Carbohydrates: 40 grams • Fiber: 6.3 grams • Fat: Total: 3.75 grams • Saturated: 0.67 gram • Cholesterol: 57.5 milligrams • Sodium: 752 milligrams

Tandoori Chicken Brochettes

Serves 6 to 8

her loves this Indian recipe because it is loaded with flavor. The secret lies in allowing the yogurt marinade to tenderize and flavor the small cubes of chicken, then cooking the chicken at an intensely high heat. Traditionally, Indians cook chicken in fiercely hot "tandoor" ovens to sear the surface and seal in the juices. I cook it on skewers under a hot broiler, achieving moist chicken without the use of oil. It makes a colorful, dramatic presentation on top of a bed of couscous or Chutney Basmati Rice (page 173).

12 (10-inch) bamboo skewers, soaked in water, or metal skewers
8 boneless, skinless chicken breast halves (about 2½ pounds), rinsed, patted dry, and cut into 1-inch cubes
3 or 4 tablespoons fresh lemon juice
1 teaspoon salt
TANDOORI MARINADE:
2 teaspoons minced garlic
1 tablespoon minced fresh ginger
2 serrano or jalapeño chiles, stems removed, seeded, and minced
1 cup plain nonfat yogurt
4 teaspoons tandoori spice mixture, sold in jars or packets in the spice section of grocery stores (see Note)

Vegetable oil cooking spray

Pierce the center of each chicken cube with a sharp knife so the marinade can easily permeate the chicken. Mix the chicken and lemon juice together in a nonmetallic bowl. Add the salt and rub it into the chicken pieces.

To prepare the marinade, combine the garlic, ginger, and chiles in a blender or food processor fitted with a metal blade. Blend until finely chopped. Add the yogurt and tandoori spice mixture and blend until smooth and a uniform reddish-orange color.

Pour the marinade over the chicken and combine thoroughly. Marinate in the refrigerator for at least 1 hour, or up to 8 hours.

Preheat an oven broiler with the shelf positioned closest to the heat. Lightly coat a baking sheet with a thin film of vegetable oil cooking spray.

Thread 6 or 7 cubes of chicken onto each skewer and place them on the sheet. Lightly coat with cooking spray. Broil 7 to 8 minutes until lightly charred or browned; no turning is necessary.

NOTE:

To make your own tandoori spice mixture: In a coffee or spice grinder, place 1 tablespoon each of cumin seeds and coriander seeds, 2 teaspoons cardamom pods (or use 1 teaspoon ground cardamom), 1 teaspoon cayenne, a 1-inch piece of cinnamon stick (the flaky, papery bark kind of cinnamon) or 1 teaspoon ground cinnamon, and 6 whole cloves (or use $1/2$ teaspoon ground cloves). Grind these spices to a fine powder and store in a small airtight jar for up to 3 months. (Traditionally, tandoori chicken is made deep red with food coloring. You may add a few drops of red food coloring when preparing the marinade, but it is not necessary, nor does it change the flavor.)

NUTRITIONAL ANALYSIS PER SERVING:
Calories: 202 • Protein: 38.9 grams • Carbohydrates: 4.34 grams • Fiber: 0.062 gram • Fat: Total: 2.07 grams • Saturated: 0.57 gram • Cholesterol: 91.9 milligrams • Sodium: 489 milligrams

Chicken Rollatini with Sun-Dried Tomatoes

Serves 8

*D*azzle *your guests, and yourself, with this easy but sophisticated presentation of fat-free chicken and vegetables rolled up and sliced at an angle to reveal a beautiful, mosaic pattern inside. I accompany the chicken with Lemon-Dill Rice (page 172) or Black-Eyed Pea Salad (page 43) and a green vegetable like steamed asparagus or spinach.*

4 medium carrots, cut into 3- to 4-inch julienne pieces
2 large stalks celery, cut into 3- to 4-inch julienne pieces
8 boneless, skinless chicken breast halves (about 2$\frac{1}{2}$ pounds),
    rinsed, patted dry, and butterflied
4 teaspoons minced garlic
3$\frac{1}{2}$ teaspoons all-purpose seasoning, such as Spike or Mrs. Dash
$\frac{1}{2}$ teaspoon freshly ground black pepper
16 to 24 whole fresh basil leaves
1 medium leek, white part only, washed and dried thoroughly,
    quartered lengthwise, and thinly sliced
1 tablespoon capers with juice
1 cup low-sodium chicken broth
2 tablespoons reconstituted and thinly sliced sun-dried tomatoes
    (see Note)
1$\frac{1}{2}$ tablespoons chopped parsley

In a small pot fitted with a steamer insert, bring a shallow amount of water to a boil. Place the carrots and celery in the steamer insert, cover, and steam 2 to 3 minutes until crisp-tender. Remove immediately and run under cold running water to stop the cooking process. Drain and set aside.

Preheat the oven to 350 degrees F.

Place the chicken breasts on a work surface, butterflied surfaces facing up. Spread 2$\frac{1}{2}$ teaspoons of the minced garlic onto the exposed (butterflied) sides of each chicken breast. Sprinkle 3 teaspoons of the vegetable seasoning and the black pepper over the breasts. Place 2 to 3 basil leaves, pressing them out flat, down the center length of each breast. Place equal amounts of the carrot and celery over the basil leaves. Roll the chicken breasts up around the vegetables and place them seam side down in a glass baking dish.

Sprinkle the remaining $\frac{1}{2}$ teaspoon of vegetable seasoning over the chicken. In a small bowl, combine the leek, capers, and the remaining 1$\frac{1}{2}$ teaspoons of garlic. Mix well and scatter over the chicken. Pour the chicken broth into the baking dish, cover with foil, and bake 30 minutes.

Remove the dish from the oven and scatter the sun-dried tomatoes and parsley over the chicken. Cover with the foil again and continue to bake for another 5 to 10 minutes until the chicken is firm and opaque.

When ready to serve, slice each chicken rollatini at an angle into 4 or 5 rounds to reveal the mosaic of vegetables inside. Fan the slices out around one side of a plate and spoon any remaining leek-caper mixture over the arranged pieces.

NOTE:

To reconstitute sun-dried tomatoes: In a small bowl, cover the tomatoes with hot water and let stand 20 minutes until they are pliable. Drain and slice.

NUTRITIONAL ANALYSIS PER SERVING:
Calories: 174 • Protein: 29 grams • Carbohydrates: 8.98 grams • Fiber: 2.06 grams • Fat: Total: 1.98 grams • Saturated: 0.564 gram • Cholesterol: 69 milligrans • Sodium: 158 milligrams

Spinach-Mushroom Stuffed Chicken

Serves 8

*T*his quick, elegant chicken entrée makes a striking presentation when sliced and fanned out on a plate to reveal its spinach and mushroom filling. Butterflied chicken breasts are seasoned, lined with a thin slice of provolone, filled with freshly steamed spinach and sautéed mushrooms, then rolled and baked with a tomato-caper mixture. I serve this dish to Cher and her guests with a simple wild rice pilaf and green beans or asparagus.

2 bags (10 ounces each) fresh leaf spinach, thoroughly washed
2 teaspoons butter
1 pound white mushrooms, rinsed, halved, and sliced
1³/₄ teaspoons garlic salt
Freshly ground black pepper
8 boneless, skinless chicken breast halves (about 2¹/₂ pounds), rinsed, patted dry, and butterflied
4 teaspoons all-purpose seasoning, such as Spike or Mrs. Dash
8 thin slices of provolone cheese
Vegetable oil cooking spray
2 large tomatoes, diced (about 3 cups)
1 medium leek, quartered lengthwise, thinly sliced crosswise, and thoroughly washed
1 tablespoon capers

Preheat oven to 375 degrees F.

Place the spinach in a large pot with just enough water to cover the bottom of the pot. Cover the pot, place over high heat, and steam the spinach until wilted, about 6 to 8 minutes. Drain the spinach in a colander and, when cool enough to handle, squeeze dry.

Melt the butter in a sauté pan over medium-high heat. Add the mushrooms and sauté until they begin to brown slightly and any liquid has reduced, about 10 to 12 minutes. Season with ¹/₄ teaspoon of the garlic salt and black pepper to taste. Set aside.

Lightly coat a large baking dish with vegetable oil cooking spray. Place the chicken breasts on a work surface, butterflied surfaces facing up. Season with the vegetable seasoning and 1 teaspoon of the garlic salt. Position 1 slice of provolone over the center of each chicken breast. Place equal amounts of the spinach and mushrooms on top of the cheese slices. Roll up the chicken breasts around the filling and place them seam side down in the baking dish.

In a small bowl, combine the tomatoes, leek, capers, the remaining ½ tea-spoon of garlic salt, and ground black pepper to taste. Pour the mixture over the chicken, cover with foil, and bake 30 minutes. Uncover the baking dish and cook the chicken another 15 minutes. Remove from the oven and allow to rest a few minutes.

To serve, slice each chicken breast at an angle into 4 or 5 slices. Fan the slices out on each plate and spoon some of the tomato-caper mixture over the arranged chicken.

NUTRITIONAL ANALYSIS PER SERVING:
Calories: 244 • Protein: 35 grams • Carbohydrates: 11 grams • Fiber: 4 grams • Fat: Total: 7 grams • Saturated: 4.6 grams • Cholesterol: 81 milligrams • Sodium: 853 milligrams

Barbecue Chicken Burgers

Serves 4

*T*hese chicken burgers, consisting of ground chicken, barbecue sauce, and seasonings, are a frequent lunch item for Cher. Many sports trainers and nutritionists have recommended this type of lean, high-protein meal to build lean muscle mass. I serve these to Cher by themselves with barbecue sauce on the side, although they are equally delicious on hamburger buns, in pita pocket bread, or on a bed of mixed greens. Dill Coleslaw (page 42) is a perfect accompaniment.

1¼ pounds ground chicken (or turkey)
⅓ cup minced onion
¼ cup chopped parsley
½ teaspoon celery salt
½ teaspoon garlic salt
1 tablespoon Woody's Cook-in sauce barbecue concentrate or your favorite barbecue sauce, plus extra to serve on the side
Vegetable oil cooking spray
4 hamburger buns, preferably onion or multigrain, split (optional)

In a small bowl, mix together the ground chicken, onion, parsley, celery salt, garlic salt, and 1 tablespoon of the barbecue sauce. Wet your hands and divide the mixture into four 5-inch round patties.

Coat the bottom of a large nonstick skillet with a thin film of vegetable oil cooking spray. Place it on the stove over medium heat. Brown the patties for about 6 minutes on one side, then turn and finish cooking them for another 5 to 6 minutes. (Don't worry if the burgers appear black or burnt—this is only the barbecue sauce caramelizing on the outside.)

Meanwhile, grill or toast the buns, if using. Serve the burgers with a small cup of extra barbecue sauce on the side.

NUTRITIONAL ANALYSIS PER SERVING (including bun):
Calories: 446 • Protein: 36.2 grams • Carbohydrates: 34.9 grams • Fiber: 0.423 gram • Fat: Total: 16.5 grams • Saturated: 3.72 grams • Cholesterol: 111 milligrams • Sodium: 862 milligrams

Cadillac Camping

One summer, we went up to Aspen for a brief getaway from the city. After a few days at the house, Cher thought it would be fun for all of us to go camping. Besides, it was July. What better way to enjoy the natural wonders around us than to go out and experience them? A terrific idea, in theory.

Well, several local friends decided to join us (just in case we didn't know what we were doing), dubbing our little adventure "Cadillac camping," meaning "urbanites roughing it." Packing for the trip was an adventure in itself. My duty was to pack the cars with all the gear. I found myself loading everything from battery-operated radios to sheepskins, pillows, and cots. Everything but the kitchen sink. By the time the cars were loaded, there was barely any room for us to squeeze in!

We drove about 15 minutes out of town to a beautiful campground surrounded by majestic mountains. As we approached the campsites, the skies suddenly darkened and the aspen trees began to sway in a howling wind. A fast-approaching mountain storm was upon us. Minutes later, before we could even set up a tent, it started to . . . not rain, but snow! Our trip was dashed, and after a few colorful expletives from Cher, we headed home in disappointment. My hot dogs and marshmallows would have to wait.

Elijah's Mustard-Caper Chicken Burgers

Serves 4

her's son, Elijah Blue, is really great in the kitchen. When he's not busy snowboarding or looking for his next tattoo design, he likes to delve into the culinary world of mixing and matching flavors. One of his best creations is this burger, combining ground chicken or turkey with Dijon mustard and capers. This has, in fact, become one of the most popular lunches in the house. Of course I love it because it is so quick and easy to prepare. These flavorful burgers are wonderful and low in fat on their own, but if you cannot imagine eating a burger without a bun, go for it! Elijah insists that the best accompaniments to his burgers are a Caesar salad and Grilled Ratatouille (page 151). I concur.

1 to 1¼ pounds ground chicken (or turkey)
¼ cup Dijon mustard
2 tablespoons capers
½ teaspoon garlic salt
½ teaspoon freshly ground black pepper
¼ cup chopped parsley
Vegetable oil cooking spray
4 hamburger buns, or slices of focaccia bread, split (optional)

In a bowl, combine the ground chicken, mustard, capers, garlic salt, black pepper, and parsley. Mix thoroughly. Wet your hands and divide the mixture into four 5-inch round patties.

Coat the bottom of a large nonstick skillet with a thin film of vegetable oil cooking spray and place on the stove over medium heat. Brown the patties on one side about 8 minutes, then turn and cook them for another 6 to 7 minutes.

Meanwhile, grill or toast the buns, if using. Serve.

NUTRITIONAL ANALYSIS PER SERVING (without bun):
Calories: 277 • Protein: 31.2 grams • Carbohydrates: 2.03 grams • Fiber: 0.5 gram • Fat: Total: 15.8 grams • Saturated: 3.77 grams • Cholesterol: 111 milligrams • Sodium: 780 milligrams

NUTRITIONAL ANALYSIS PER SERVING (with bun):
Calories: 457 • Protein: 37 grams • Carbohydrates: 35 grams • Fiber: 0.5 gram • Fat: Total: 17.8 grams • Saturated: 3.8 grams • Cholesterol: 111 milligrams • Sodium: 1225 milligrams

No-Fat Homemade Gravy

Makes 3 ¹/₄ cups

*N*o guilt, no compromising on taste, and no lumps with this gravy. Typically, gravy is made from the rendered fat that "melts" off a roasted meat or bird. This saturated, "hard" fat, visible on all meat and in the skin of poultry, is the worst fat for you, so I devised this no-fat gravy, which can be made with chicken or vegetable broth. This recipe cooks quickly and, after being puréed in a blender, results in a delicious, thick gravy that looks and tastes just like its high-fat counterpart. It is excellent over mashed potatoes, shepherd's pie, turkey meat loaf, or roasted turkey and Georgia's Corn Bread Dressing (page 167).

1 small onion, thinly sliced
²/₃ cup sliced carrots
¹/₃ cup sliced celery
1 large tomato, peeled, seeded (see sidebar, page 77), and coarsely chopped
3 cloves peeled garlic
1 can (14¹/₂ ounces) low-sodium chicken or vegetable broth
Pinch of dried rubbed sage
Pinch of dried thyme
Pinch of dried rosemary
¹/₄ teaspoon salt
Freshly ground black pepper

In a medium saucepan, combine all of the ingredients and bring to a boil. Reduce the heat and simmer, covered, until the vegetables are soft, about 25 minutes. Remove from the stove.

Pour the entire contents of the saucepan into a blender. Purée until smooth. (Be careful when puréeing not to fill the blender more than two-thirds full, as the hot liquid may splash out and burn you. Placing a large kitchen towel over the machine before operating helps to avoid such an accident.) Adjust seasoning with additional salt or freshly ground black pepper to taste. (The gravy may be prepared ahead to this point and reheated just before serving.)

Serve hot in a gravy boat with a ladle, or in a small pitcher.

NUTRITIONAL ANALYSIS PER ¹/₂-CUP SERVING:
Calories: 27.0 • Protein: 1.44 grams • Carbohydrates: 4.93 grams • Fiber: 1.13 grams • Fat: Total: 0.652 grams • Saturated: 0.283 gram • Cholesterol: 1.29 milligrams • Sodium: 129 milligrams

Meats

Beef Meatballs in an Herbed Olive Marinara Sauce

Serves 8, with leftovers

When I was little, I thought there was nothing like the aroma of my grandmother's meatballs wafting throughout the house before dinnertime. They gave me such a voracious appetite that when I did sit down for dinner I tried to fit as much as possible in my mouth at one time. I'll never forget my mother grabbing the kitchen scissors and snipping off the lengths of spaghetti dangling from my mouth! My eating habits have much improved since, but my love affair with meatballs continues.

In an effort to reduce some of the oil used in preparing meatballs, I now broil them in the oven. They brown just as well, and the cleanup is much easier. I also make my own bread crumbs, from sturdy bread like a crusty Italian or sourdough loaf, because the store-bought crumbs contain so much more fat. Neither of these procedures compromises taste, so when you try these meatballs simmered slowly in sauce, maybe you will share my childhood passion.

OLIVE MARINARA SAUCE:
    2 teaspoons extra-virgin olive oil
    2 medium onions, chopped
    1 tablespoon minced garlic
    1 can (28 ounces) Italian-style whole tomatoes and liquid, the
        tomatoes cut up
    1 can (28 ounces) tomato purée
    2 tablespoons red wine
    1/4 cup oil-cured black olives, pitted and roughly chopped
    2 teaspoons crushed dried basil
    1/2 teaspoon crushed dried oregano
    1 bay leaf
    Pinch of cayenne
    1 tablespoon sugar

    Vegetable oil cooking spray
MEATBALLS:
    2 1/2 cups fresh bread crumbs
    1 cup low-fat milk, beef broth, or water
    1 1/2 pounds lean ground beef (preferably not exceeding 10% fat)
    1 egg or 2 egg whites, beaten
    1 small onion, finely chopped

1 tablespoon minced garlic

1/4 cup chopped parsley

1 teaspoon crushed dried oregano

2 teaspoons crushed dried basil

1/2 teaspoon salt

1/2 teaspoon freshly ground black pepper

1 tablespoon grated Parmesan cheese, plus extra to pass at the table, if you wish

3/4 pound fedelini or spaghettini pasta

To prepare the sauce: Heat the olive oil in a 5-quart pot over medium-high heat. Sauté the onions and garlic until softened and beginning to brown, about 5 minutes. Add the cut-up tomatoes, tomato purée, red wine, olives, basil, oregano, bay leaf, cayenne, and sugar. Bring to a gentle boil, reduce the heat, and slowly simmer, covered, for 25 minutes, stirring occasionally. Remove the bay leaf.

Preheat the oven broiler and position the shelf on the second level from the broiler. Coat a baking sheet with a thin film of vegetable oil cooking spray. Set aside.

To prepare the meatballs: Soak the bread crumbs in the milk in a large bowl. Add the beef and egg and knead until fully incorporated. Add all of the remaining ingredients (except the pasta) and knead until thoroughly combined.

To shape the meatballs, wet your hands and, using about 1 heaping tablespoon of meat mixture for each, form walnut-size balls. Place the meatballs on the prepared baking sheet. Broil them until brown on one side, about 6 to 8 minutes. Turn and repeat. When they are browned, remove the meatballs from the broiler and set in a colander to drain any excess fat. Add the meatballs to the sauce and simmer 30 to 40 minutes.

Meanwhile, bring a pot of salted water to a boil and cook the pasta according to package directions until al dente. Drain.

Serve the pasta in bowls with the meatballs and sauce spooned over each serving. If desired, pass additional grated Parmesan at the table.

NUTRITIONAL ANALYSIS PER SERVING:
Calories: 576 • Protein: 32.9 grams • Carbohydrates: 77.5 grams • Fiber: 6.56 grams • Fat: Total: 14.6 grams • Saturated: 4.87 grams • Cholesterol: 61.6 milligrams • Sodium: 1150 milligrams

Beef Stew and Vegetables

Serves 6

I have cooked countless versions of stews over the years, and have combined the best results of each in this recipe. The first thing to keep in mind in cooking a stew is how uncomplicated a preparation it is for such a grand result. Treat the meat tenderly while you brown it, and allow several hours of slow simmering; you will be rewarded with a rich, brown, hearty stew.

In my efforts to keep fat to a minimum, I purchase a whole beef chuck pot roast and cube it myself. This way, I can remove most of the fat, and since the meat all comes from the same cut, it will cook uniformly.

It is my experience that the best results come from initial browning, or cara-melizing, of the meat. Be patient, as this is the most important step, and it will only take about 10 to 15 minutes. Be careful not to crowd the pan, or the meat will boil in its own juices instead of browning. The stew is then braised in the oven at a low temperature for several hours until tender. This stew may be prepared several days in advance, which will improve and intensify its flavor.

At Cher's home, I accompany the beef stew with Horseradish Mashed Potatoes (page 163) or parsleyed noodles. Also, green beans or broccoli steamed crisp-tender work beautifully to contrast with the tender meat.

2½ pounds beef chuck, cut into 1-inch cubes trimmed of any fat
½ teaspoon salt
½ teaspoon freshly ground black pepper
4 teaspoons vegetable oil
2 medium onions, coarsely chopped
1 tablespoon plus 1 teaspoon minced garlic
3 tablespoons flour
1 cup red wine, such as a California Cabernet, zinfandel, or Chianti
1 can (14½ ounces) beef broth
½ cup low-sodium tomato juice
½ teaspoon dried thyme
Pinch of ground cloves
Pinch of ground ginger
1 bay leaf

6 to 8 medium carrots, cut into ³/₄-inch chunks
3 stalks celery, cut into ³/₄-inch chunks
1 medium rutabaga, peeled and cut into ³/₄-inch cubes
1 bag (10 ounces) frozen pearl onions, cooked according to package
     directions
3 tablespoons chopped parsley

Preheat the oven to 300 degrees F.

Place the beef cubes in a large bowl and sprinkle with the salt and pepper. To brown the beef properly, it will be necessary to cook it in two batches. Using a large nonstick sauté pan, heat 2 teaspoons of the vegetable oil over medium-high heat and add half of the meat, without crowding the pan. Allow the beef to brown nicely on one side before turning. Brown all sides, about 7 minutes total. Turn out the browned meat cubes into a 15 x 10 x 12-inch (4-quart) glass or enameled baking dish. Add the remaining 2 teaspoons of oil and repeat the browning process with the second batch of beef; add it to the baking dish. Do not rinse out the pan.

Reduce the heat to medium. Add the onions to the pan and sauté until softened, about 5 minutes. Add the garlic and continue to sauté for a few seconds. Stir in the flour and cook 1 to 2 minutes. The mixture will be quite dry, because of the little amount of fat in the pan.

Deglaze by adding the wine and scraping the flavorful, browned bits from the bottom of the pan. Add the beef broth, tomato juice, thyme, cloves, ginger, and bay leaf. Bring to a simmer. The mixture should have a rich, brown, saucelike consistency. Pour the liquid over the meat in the baking dish. Cover tightly with aluminum foil and place in the oven for about 1 hour.

Remove the dish from the oven and add the carrots, celery, and rutabaga. Cover and return the dish to the oven. Continue to braise the stew another 1¹/₂ hours. Remove the dish from the oven, add the pearl onions, cover, and braise 30 minutes longer. Finally remove the stew from the oven, remove the bay leaf, stir in the parsley, adjust the seasonings, and serve.

NUTRITIONAL ANALYSIS PER SERVING:
Calories: 478 • Protein: 51.6 grams • Carbohydrates: 25.2 grams • Fiber: 5.11 grams • Fat: Total: 15.5 grams • Saturated: 4.6 grams • Cholesterol: 145 milligrams • Sodium: 666 milligrams

Stuffed Grape Leaves (Dolmas)

Makes 25 stuffed grape leaves; serves 6

her tells me she has loved grape leaves ever since her mother intro-duced them to her when she was young. Grape leaves come packed in brine liquid, which is drained and the leaves are rinsed when this recipe is prepared. The leaves are then laid flat, undersides up, and are stuffed with a ground beef and uncooked rice mixture. The leaves are then rolled like a cigar around the stuffing and cooked in a beefy tomato sauce. I often prepare these ahead of time, since they reheat beautifully and are very good cold as well.

This recipe was adapted from the esteemed Craig Claiborne, in The New York Times Cookbook *(1961).*

1$\frac{1}{2}$ pounds extra-lean (7% fat) ground beef
$\frac{3}{4}$ cup raw long-grain white rice
1 small onion, grated (about $\frac{1}{2}$ cup)
$\frac{3}{4}$ teaspoon dried thyme
$\frac{1}{2}$ teaspoon crushed dried oregano
$\frac{1}{3}$ cup chopped parsley
$\frac{1}{4}$ cup snipped fresh dill
$\frac{1}{4}$ teaspoon freshly ground black pepper
$\frac{1}{4}$ teaspoon salt
1 can (14$\frac{1}{2}$ ounces) beef broth
1 can (16 ounces) tomato purée
1 can (15 ounces) tomato sauce
1 jar (8 ounces) grape leaves, rinsed and drained

Preheat oven to 350 degrees F.

In a bowl, mix together the beef, rice, onion, thyme, oregano, parsley, dill, black pepper, and salt.

In a separate bowl, combine the beef broth, tomato purée, and tomato sauce. Add 1$\frac{1}{2}$ cups of this sauce to the meat mixture. Pour another 2 cups of sauce into the bottom of a 15 x 10 x 2-inch (4-quart) glass or enameled baking dish. Reserve the remaining sauce for later use.

Separate a few grape leaves at a time and lay flat, undersides up, on a work surface. Place about 2 to 3 tablespoons of meat filling on each leaf and roll them into elongated cigar shapes, tucking in the sides as you roll them. Place each rolled leaf seam side down in the baking dish containing the sauce.

Pour the remaining sauce over the top. Cover the dish tightly with aluminum foil and bake until the rice in the filling is fully cooked (you will have to cut into one to check) and the sauce has thickened slightly, about 1 to 1¼ hours.

NUTRITIONAL ANALYSIS PER SERVING:
Calories: 367 • Protein: 29.9 grams • Carbohydrates: 38 grams • Fiber: 3.48 grams • Fat: Total: 11 grams • Saturated: 4.22 grams • Cholesterol: 41.3 milligrams • Sodium: 1136 milligrams

Andy and Cher in the kitchen of the ocean house.

Chef on a Harley.

Andy's Greek Tomato Salad begins a dinner for eight.

Andy demonstrating his cooking technique.

Andy prepares vegetable lasagna.

Christmas, 1992. Cher and her sister Georganne in Aspen.

Cher's birthday cake, 1989.

Cher and Elijah Blue.

Cher's mom, Georgia, Andy, and Chastity.

Fajita Skirt Steak

Serves 6

I call this my *"fajita marinade"*; it lends a real Southwest flavor to beef and is also excellent used on grilled onions and peppers. It contains lime juice, which not only brings a bright flavor to beef but also has a tenderizing effect. Even though the skirt steak will cook in just minutes, begin marinating the beef up to 2 hours in advance in order to bring out the best flavors. This steak and the grilled vegetables, if served in the traditional fajita style, would include warmed tortillas, salsa, and low- or nonfat sour cream.

> 2 tablespoons extra-virgin olive oil
> 1/4 cup fresh lime juice, rinds reserved and quartered (about 2 to 3 limes)
> 2 fresh medium jalapeño chiles, seeded and coarsely chopped
> 1/3 cup coarsely chopped cilantro
> 1 tablespoon sliced garlic
> 2 teaspoons ground cumin
> 1 1/2 teaspoons chili powder
> 1 1/2 teaspoons garlic salt
> 1/2 teaspoon Mexican oregano
> Pinch of crushed red pepper
> 1 3/4 pounds beef loin skirt steaks, trimmed of any fat
> 1 large red onion, cut into 1/2-inch-thick rounds
> 1 red bell pepper, seeded and cut into large strips
> 1 yellow bell pepper, seeded and cut into large strips

Combine the olive oil, lime juice and rinds, jalapeño, cilantro, garlic, cumin, chili powder, garlic salt, oregano, and crushed red pepper in a large, shallow, nonreactive dish. Mix well.

Add the skirt steaks one at a time, thoroughly rubbing each steak with the marinade so it permeates the meat. Allow to marinate, covered and refrigerated, for up to 2 hours. Add the onion and peppers and rub with the marinade.

Preheat a hot barbecue grill. (Alternatively, preheat the oven broiler with the shelf positioned closest to the heat.) Grill the steaks, along with the vegetables, on one side until marked and charred, about 3 to 4 minutes. Then turn the steaks and vegetables and continue to grill to desired doneness. (If broiling, place the steaks and vegetables on a baking sheet in a single layer and broil to desired doneness, turning once.)

Slice the steaks across the grain into thin strips. Serve the steak and grilled vegetables on a warm platter.

VARIATIONS AND SUGGESTIONS:

Lime Chicken: The lime marinade is just as delicious used for chicken. Simply substitute about 2 pounds of boneless, skinless chicken breasts for the steak. Marinate the chicken only 30 minutes, then grill until firm, about 12 to 15 minutes, turning once. The lime chicken may be used sliced on salads (like Caesar or spinach), in burritos, or in tacos. Or chop the chicken and float it on top of Spicy Corn Chowder (page 56).

NUTRITIONAL ANALYSIS PER SERVING (does not include tortilla, salsa, or sour cream):
Calories: 241 • Protein: 27.1 grams • Carbohydrates: 3.76 grams • Fiber: 0.783 gram • Fat: Total: 12.3 grams • Saturated: 4.61 grams • Cholesterol: 66.2 milligrams • Sodium: 207 milligrams

Pork, Hominy, and Green Chile Stew

Serves 8 to 10

oblano chiles give this stew its spicy character. These shiny, dark-green chiles are about 5 inches long, with a tapered pointy shape, and can be mild to somewhat hot. The pork in this stew gets a melt-in-your-mouth quality from long, slow cooking in a rather unconventional green chile purée.

1 can (27 ounces) mild, whole green chiles
1 tablespoon extra-virgin olive oil
3 medium onions, roughly chopped
3³/₄ pounds boneless pork loin roast, trimmed of all fat and cut into
  ¹/₂-inch cubes (3¹/₃ pounds trimmed)
4¹/₂ tablespoons chopped garlic
¹/₂ teaspoon freshly ground black pepper
1 tablespoon ground cumin
2 teaspoons crushed Mexican oregano
1 teaspoon whole cumin seed
4 or 5 roasted poblano chiles, cut into ¹/₂-inch squares
2 cans (14¹/₂ ounces each) low-sodium chicken broth
2 cans (29¹/₂ ounces each) Mexican-style hominy, rinsed and drained
¹/₂ teaspoon salt
2 tablespoons chopped cilantro, plus extra for garnish

Rinse and drain the canned green chiles. Purée them in a blender or food processor fitted with a metal blade until very smooth. Set aside.

Heat the olive oil in a large pot. Sauté the onions over high heat until translucent, about 5 minutes. Add the pork, garlic, black pepper, ground cumin, oregano, and cumin seed. Cook for about 6 minutes, or until the pork becomes opaque.

Add the green chile purée, poblano chile pieces, chicken broth, hominy, and salt. Bring to a boil, reduce the heat, and simmer, covered, about 2 hours, or until the pork is tender and the stew has thickened. Stir occasionally.

Stir in the cilantro and cook another few minutes. Adjust the seasoning, if necessary, with more salt or black pepper to taste. Serve garnished with cilantro.

NUTRITIONAL ANALYSIS PER SERVING:
Calories: 478 • Protein: 47.5 grams • Carbohydrates: 33 grams • Fiber: 4.14 grams • Fat: Total: 16.7 grams • Saturated: 5.43 grams • Cholesterol: 115 milligrams • Sodium: 688 milligrams

Albondigas in a Tomato-Orange Sauce (Mexican Meatballs)

Serves 6 to 8

*T*he bright flavors of this Mexican specialty make this one of my favorite meals. The meatballs, each studded with a green olive in the center, are a pleasing contrast to the brothy tomato sauce in which oranges, skin and all, are cooked. As the oranges simmer in the sauce, the meatballs begin to take on the subtle citrus flavors.

For best flavor combination and visual presentation, I serve the albondigas *over my Vibrant Verde Rice (page 171). The rice, which contains roasted poblano chiles and fresh cilantro, perfectly complements the* albondigas, *although regular white rice will work as well. Any leftovers are wonderful wrapped in a heated tortilla with shredded lettuce.*

$^1/_2$ cup raw long-grain white rice

TOMATO-ORANGE SAUCE:
  1 tablespoon vegetable or peanut oil
  $3^1/_2$ cups chopped onion
  3 tablespoons minced garlic
  $^1/_2$ teaspoon whole cumin seed
  2 cans (28 ounces each) whole tomatoes and liquid, puréed
  1 can ($14^1/_2$ ounces) low-sodium chicken broth
  2 small navel oranges, quartered
  $^1/_2$ teaspoon ground cumin
  $^1/_2$ teaspoon salt, or more

MEATBALLS:
  3 slices sturdy white bread, soaked in water, lightly squeezed, and
    drained
  1 pound lean ground pork
  1 pound lean ground beef
  1 egg or 2 egg whites
  $1^1/_2$ tablespoons minced garlic
  $^3/_4$ teaspoon crushed dried Mexican oregano
  1 teaspoon ground cumin
  $^1/_2$ teaspoon salt
  $^1/_4$ teaspoon freshly ground black pepper
  25 small Spanish green olives stuffed with pimento, halved widthwise

In a small pot, parboil the rice with 1 cup of water until it is almost cooked, about 10 to 12 minutes. Drain any excess liquid, set aside, and allow to cool.

In the meantime, prepare the Tomato-Orange Sauce by heating the oil in a large, wide pot over medium heat. Add the onion and sauté until softened, about 4 minutes. Add the garlic and cumin seed and continue to cook another 1 to 2 minutes.

Add the puréed tomatoes, chicken broth, oranges (squeezed slightly), cumin, and salt. Bring to a boil, reduce the heat, and gently simmer, uncovered, about 15 minutes.

While the sauce simmers, prepare the meatball mixture. In a large mixing bowl, combine the soaked bread, ground pork, ground beef, egg, garlic, oregano, cumin, salt, and pepper. Thoroughly mix the rice into the meat mixture.

To shape the meatballs, wet your hands and take out enough meat mixture to form into walnut-size balls. You should have about 50 meatballs. Poke a green olive into the center of each meatball formed and drop them into the simmering sauce. Once all the meatballs have been added to the sauce, remove and discard all of the orange wedges using a slotted spoon. Cover the pot and simmer another 25 minutes, gently stirring once or twice. The sauce should have the consistency of a thin, brothlike tomato sauce. If it is too thin, continue to simmer uncovered until some of the liquid cooks off. Adjust seasoning, if necessary.

NUTRITIONAL ANALYSIS PER SERVING:
Calories: 545 • Protein: 41 grams • Carbohydrates: 48 grams • Fiber: 5.5 grams • Fat: Total: 22 grams • Saturated: 7 grams • Cholesterol: 103 milligrams • Sodium: 1316 milligrams

Vegetarian Main Courses

Lentil Chili

Serves 6

*T*hese slowly simmered lentils have a rich, meaty flavor spiced with cumin and chili powder. The high fiber content of lentils make this wintertime meal healthy and filling, especially if it is served with Mexican Corn Bread (page 170), Vibrant Verde Rice (page 171) or hot corn tortillas, and Cher's Ranch Salad (page 31).

2 teaspoons extra-virgin olive oil
1 large onion, chopped
1 tablespoon minced garlic
1 pound (about 2½ cups) dried brown lentils, picked over and rinsed
15 ounces canned tomato sauce
1 can (16 ounces) diced tomatoes and liquid
2 tablespoons chili powder
1 tablespoon ground cumin
1 teaspoon ground coriander
¼ teaspoon cayenne
4¾ cups water or vegetable broth

GARNISHES:

¼ cup grated soy cheese or low-fat Cheddar cheese (optional)
1 large ripe tomato, diced
2 roasted poblano or Anaheim green chile peppers (see page 157), diced, or 2 ounces canned mild green chiles, rinsed and diced
3 tablespoons coarsely chopped cilantro (optional)
¼ cup nonfat or low-fat sour cream (optional)

Heat the oil in a 4-quart pot over medium heat and sauté the onion and garlic until soft, about 5 minutes. Stir in the lentils. Add the tomato sauce, diced tomatoes, spices, and vegetable broth. Bring to a boil, reduce the heat, and simmer, covered, until the lentils are tender, about 1 hour. The mixture should be thick.

Garnish the chili with whichever additions you choose: a sprinkling of grated cheese, diced tomato, green chiles, cilantro, and/or a dollop of the sour cream.

NUTRITIONAL ANALYSIS PER SERVING (without garnishes):
Calories: 332 • Protein: 24.6 grams • Carbohydrates: 56.9 grams • Fiber: 12.6 grams • Fat: Total: 2.62 grams • Saturated: 0.363 gram • Cholesterol: 0 • Sodium: 561 milligrams

Vegetable-Stuffed Potatoes

Serves 4 as an entrée,
8 as a side dish

*W*hat food is more fun than twice-baked potatoes; the tender flesh billowing out of the skins like puffy clouds? The first time I served these to Cher, she asked if I could prepare them mixed with her favorite vegetables. So the next time around, I baked and mashed the potatoes, then added spinach, corn, and roasted red bell peppers (although nearly any combination of vegetables will work fine) for a huge hit.

If you want to serve these as a side dish, simply cut the potatoes in half after baking, rather than just cutting the tops off. This way you will get twice as many stuffed potatoes in smaller portions.

4 medium Idaho potatoes (about 3³/₄ pounds)
1 cup nonfat milk, warmed
¹/₄ teaspoon salt
¹/₄ teaspoon garlic salt
2 teaspoons butter
³/₄ cup sliced green onions
1 bunch spinach (³/₄ pound), stemmed, thoroughly washed, dried, and
   cut up (see page 65)
1 cup fresh or frozen corn
1 roasted red bell pepper (see page 37), cut into strips; or 1 jar
   (4 ounces) sliced pimientos, drained
¹/₄ cup grated low-fat Cheddar cheese (optional)

Preheat the oven to 375 degrees F.

Place the potatoes in the oven and bake until soft when pierced with a fork, about 1¹/₄ hours. Remove from the oven and, when cool enough to handle, cut an ellipse out of the top of each potato. Using a spoon, scoop out the pulp into a bowl, leaving ¹/₄-inch potato pulp. Set aside the hollow potato skins for stuffing later.

Reduce the oven temperature to 350 degrees F.

Using an electric mixer or hand-held potato masher, lightly break up the potatoes. Gradually add the milk and mash the potatoes until all of the liquid is absorbed and the potatoes are light and fluffy. Mix in the salt, garlic salt, and 1 teaspoon of the butter. Set aside.

In a large sauté pan over medium heat, melt the remaining 1 teaspoon of butter and lightly sauté the green onions, spinach leaves, and corn just until the spinach has wilted, a few minutes. Drain any excess liquid. Add the vegetables to the mashed potatoes, along with the roasted red bell pepper.

Stuff the vegetable-potato mixture into the hollow potato skins. Top each potato with a sprinkling of the Cheddar cheese, if using. Return the stuffed potatoes to the oven and bake until heated through and lightly browned, about 25 minutes. Serve hot.

These potatoes make a wonderful lunch or dinner served with soup or a mixed green salad.

VARIATIONS AND SUGGESTIONS:
For a unique variation, try adding Greek olives and feta cheese, or use green chiles for a spicy flair.

NUTRITIONAL ANALYSIS PER SERVING (based on 4 servings per recipe):
Calories: 564 • Protein: 16.1 grams • Carbohydrates: 123 grams • Fiber: 14.4 grams • Fat: Total: 3.28 grams • Saturated: 1.51 grams • Cholesterol: 6.28 milligrams • Sodium: 359 milligrams

Potato Frankies

Makes 8 filled crêpes; serves 8 as an entrée

Frankies were first introduced in Bombay about twenty years ago and could be thought of as the Indian version of frankfurters, although they are quite different. Today Indian streets are dotted with pushcarts offering this favorite fast food, served in its own edible carrying case.

If you haven't yet experimented with Indian cuisine, this flavorful mélange of vegetables spiced with curry, crystallized ginger, and chiles, all enclosed in a burrito-like wrapper, could make you a diehard fan.

CURRY CRÊPE BATTER:
1 cup sifted all-purpose flour
2 extra-large eggs
1 1/2 cups nonfat milk
1/2 teaspoon sugar
1/4 teaspoon salt
2 tablespoons chopped parsley
1 tablespoon chopped fresh mint leaves
2 teaspoons safflower oil
2 teaspoons curry powder

Vegetable oil cooking spray, for cooking the crêpes

POTATO FILLING:
3 large Idaho or russet potatoes (2 3/4 to 3 pounds), peeled and cut into 1/2-inch dice
1 teaspoon salt
1 small head caulifower (about 1 1/2 pounds), cut into florets
1 tablespoon butter
1 1/2 cups finely diced onion
1 teaspoon cumin
2 tablespoons curry powder
1 tablespoon plus 1 teaspoon seeded and minced serrano chiles (4 or 5)
1/2 cup low-fat coconut milk, skimmed of any fat
1/2 cup vegetable broth or water
2 tablespoons finely chopped crystallized ginger
2 tablespoons chopped fresh mint leaves

Mango chutney, served as a condiment

To prepare the batter: In a small bowl, combine the flour, eggs, milk, sugar, salt, parsley, and mint, mixing with a fork until smooth. Cover and refrigerate for 1 hour.

Meanwhile, heat the oil in a small pan over low heat. Add the curry powder and cook 2 to 3 minutes, until fragrant. Cool. Stir into the batter; it will turn a brilliant yellow.

In a medium pot, bring the diced potatoes, 1 quart of water, and the salt to a boil. Reduce the heat and simmer the potatoes until just tender (still holding their shape but not mushy), about 10 to 15 minutes. Drain and set aside.

Steam the cauliflower until tender, about 8 to 10 minutes. Cool under cold running water. Drain, chop coarsely, and set aside.

In a large, wide pot or dutch oven, melt the butter over medium heat. Add the onion and sauté until soft and translucent. Add the cumin and curry powder and cook until fragrant, 1 to 2 minutes. Add the serrano chiles, coconut milk, vegetable broth, crystallized ginger, and mint. Reduce the heat and simmer, covered, for 8 to 10 minutes. Add the potatoes and cauliflower, stirring until all ingredients are thoroughly mixed. The filling should be dense and thick. More liquid, either water or broth, may be added if it is too dry. Season with additional salt, if needed. Cover the pot and keep the filling warm until ready to spoon into the crêpes.

To make the crêpes, preheat a 12-inch nonstick skillet over medium heat. Coat with a thin film of vegetable oil cooking spray. Ladle 3 tablespoons of the batter into one side of the skillet and quickly swirl the batter around to coat the entire bottom of the pan. Cook until bubbles appear and the edges begin to dry and curl, then turn the crêpe over and cook the other side half as long. The crêpe should be thin and a brilliant yellow speckled with light brown spots. Place on a large plate and continue cooking crêpes in the same manner, inserting waxed paper between cooked crêpes, until you have used all the batter.

Spoon about ³/₄ cup of warm potato filling onto one half of each crêpe. Roll up, tucking the sides in so the crêpes somewhat resemble rolled burritos. Serve with the mango chutney on the side.

VARIATIONS AND SUGGESTIONS:
For smaller "frankies" to serve as hors d'oeuvres at large parties or brunches, prepare the crêpes in a smaller, 8-inch nonstick skillet. Fill each crêpe with only ¹/₃ cup potato filling, thereby making about 16 to 18 "frankies."

NUTRITIONAL ANALYSIS PER SERVING:
Calories: 323 • Protein: 10.7 grams • Carbohydrates: 58.3 grams • Fiber: 5.64 grams • Fat: Total: 6.43 grams • Saturated: 3.17 grams • Cholesterol: 57.7 milligrams • Sodium: 229 milligrams

Rustic Grilled Tomato Sauce and Pasta

Serves 6 to 8

*T*his is a wonderful, rather chunky sauce to put over any pasta, and is excellent as an accompaniment to Olive Tapenade Chicken (page 95). Lots of fresh herbs with olive oil are brushed over tomatoes and onions, which are grilled. Then the tomatoes and onions are coarsely chopped, becoming the base ingredients to make this sauce. The grilling produces sweet and smoky flavors that make this incomparable.

GRILLED TOMATOES:
1 tablespoon extra-virgin olive oil
2 tablespoons coarsely chopped garlic
2 tablespoons coarsely chopped fresh oregano
2 tablespoons coarsely chopped fresh marjoram
1 teaspoon kosher salt
$^1/_2$ teaspoon freshly ground black pepper
2 medium red onions, cut into $^1/_2$-inch-thick round slices
$3^1/_2$ pounds plum tomatoes, peeled, halved crosswise, seeds removed (see page 77)

SAUCE:
1 teaspoon extra-virgin olive oil
2 cups tomato purée
2 tablespoons red wine
1 bay leaf
2 teaspoons coarsely chopped basil
Pinch of cayenne
1 teaspoon sugar
2 teaspoons salt
$^1/_3$ cup oil-cured black olives, pitted and roughly chopped

1 pound angel-hair (capellini) pasta

To prepare the tomatoes: Preheat a barbecue grill to medium-hot. (Alternatively, preheat the oven broiler, with the shelf adjusted to the middle level.)

In a small bowl, combine the olive oil with the garlic, oregano, marjoram, salt, and pepper. Mix well.

Arrange the onions and tomatoes on a baking sheet in a single layer. Using the herbed oil, coat all the surfaces of the onions and tomatoes. Stuff any loose herbs into the hollow tomato cavities.

Using a metal spatula, transfer the tomatoes and onions to the grill rack and grill until lighly charred, turning once. (Alternatively, place the baking sheet containing the onions and tomatoes under the broiler and broil until the tops of the tomatoes begin to dry out and the onions begin to char slightly, about 10 minutes.) Coarsely chop the onions and tomatoes. Set aside.

In a medium pot, heat the 1 teaspoon of olive oil and sauté the chopped tomato and onion mixture for 3 to 4 minutes. Add the tomato purée, red wine, 1 cup water, the bay leaf, basil, cayenne, and sugar. Bring to a gentle boil, reduce the heat, cover the pot, and simmer slowly, 35 to 45 minutes, until a saucelike consistency is reached. Stir occasionally.

In the meantime, bring a large pot of water to a boil and add salt.

When the sauce is ready, remove the bay leaf. In a blender or food processor fitted with a metal blade, purée 2 cups of sauce until smooth. (Be careful when puréeing, as the hot liquid may splash out and burn you. Placing a large kitchen towel over the machine before operating helps in avoiding such an accident.) Return the purée to the pot of sauce. Add the olives and stir. Keep warm. (The sauce may be prepared ahead to this point.)

Plunge the pasta into the boiling water and cook until just before it reaches al dente (angel-hair pasta overcooks very quickly). Drain and serve at once in individual bowls, with the tomato sauce ladled over each serving. (If you do not plan to serve the pasta right away, it helps to mix some of the tomato sauce into the pasta to prevent it from sticking together.)

NUTRITIONAL ANALYSIS PER SERVING:
Calories: 448 • Protein: 13.9 grams • Carbohydrates: 83.0 grams • Fiber: 7.47 grams • Fat: Total: 7.25 grams • Saturated: 0.886 gram • Cholesterol: 0 • Sodium: 753 milligrams

Stir-Fried Vegetables with Yakisoba Noodles

Serves 4 to 6

f you have ever tried Chinese pan-fried noodles, you know the wonderful contrasting textures of these silky noodles, lightly browned and crisped by pan-frying in heavy amounts of oil. I have considerably reduced the amount of fat in these noodles by broiling them to achieve the same crisped effect. The broiled noodles are then combined with a colorful array of stir-fried vegetables and seasoned with a sesame teriyaki sauce. For anyone who likes pasta and Chinese food, this is it. Sorry, you have to provide your own fortune cookie.

1 package (12 ounces) yakisoba/chow mein noodles (fresh Chinese noodles in the refrigerated section of most grocery stores)
Vegetable oil cooking spray
2 tablespoons sesame teriyaki sauce
1 1/2 teaspoons spicy Sichuan stir-fry sauce (in oriental section of grocery store)
1/4 teaspoon dark sesame oil
1/2 teaspoon peanut oil
3/4 cup broccoli florets
1/8 pound snow peas, strings removed, peas sliced into thirds (about 1/2 cup)
1 small carrot, cut into short julienne pieces
1 small red bell pepper, cut into short julienne pieces
1 stalk celery, thinly sliced
1/4 pound bok choy, washed and thinly sliced, white stem and green leaves kept separate
1 cup cleaned and sliced shiitake mushrooms (soaked in hot water to reconstitute if dried)
1 tablespoon minced garlic
1 tablespoon finely chopped fresh ginger
1/3 cup thinly sliced green onions, plus extra for garnish
1 cup bean sprouts
1 can (2 3/4 ounces) baby corn, rinsed, drained, and halved lengthwise
1 can (8 ounces) sliced water chestnuts, rinsed and drained
1/4 teaspoon sea salt
2 teaspoons toasted sesame seeds, for garnish

To cook the noodles, bring 4 quarts of water to a boil. Remove the fresh noodles from their package and, with your fingers, pull apart any that may be stuck together. Put the noodles in the pot of boiling water and boil for 6 minutes. Drain in a colander, rinse well with cold water, and reserve.

Preheat the oven broiler and position the shelf on the second level down from the top of the oven. Coat a baking sheet with a thin film of the vegetable oil cooking spray.

Place the drained noodles in a bowl and mix in the sesame teriyaki sauce, spicy Sichuan stir-fry sauce, and sesame oil. Spread the noodles out over the baking sheet and lightly spray their tops with cooking spray. Broil for 6 to 8 minutes, until they begin to crisp and turn brown. Turn the mass of noodles and broil another few minutes until the majority of the noodles are browned. Turn the oven off, cover the noodles with foil, and keep warm.

Heat a nonstick wok or large sauté pan over high heat. Coat the pan with cooking spray and add the peanut oil. (For effective stir-frying, vegetables should just fill the pan in a single layer. Any larger amount will steam the vegetables rather than brown them. Depending on the size of your pan, you may need to divide and cook the vegetables in 2 batches so they will brown properly.) Add the broccoli, snow peas, carrot, red bell pepper, celery, the white stems of bok choy, and mushrooms. Stir-fry 5 minutes, tossing the vegetables only once, so they will brown properly. Add the garlic, ginger, and scallions, and toss again. Add the green leaves of the bok choy, the bean sprouts, baby corn, and water chestnuts. Stir-fry another 2 to 3 minutes until the bok choy leaves and bean sprouts wilt and all the ingredients are sufficiently heated through. Season with salt.

Combine the warm noodles with the stir-fried vegetables and add any additional sauces to taste. Serve immediately in large bowls with chopsticks. Garnish with toasted sesame seeds and thinly sliced green onions.

NUTRITIONAL ANALYSIS PER SERVING:
Calories: 286 • Protein: 7.08 grams • Carbohydrates: 61.1 grams • Fiber: 5.52 grams • Fat: Total: 2.37 grams • Saturated: 0.340 gram • Cholesterol: 0.010 milligram • Sodium: 531 milligrams

Cher and Her
"Submissive" Snow Peas

Being the chef that I am, concerned with nutrition and presentation as well as taste, I often cook green vegetables crisp-tender so they retain their nutrients and vibrant color. Cher likes all of her vegetables to be cooked to smithereens—lifeless and falling apart, but she does not always get me to go along with her.

One night for Cher's dinner I served a mélange of crisply cooked vegetables, including snow peas, to my boss, only to be summoned back into the room moments later. I thought, "How great is this? I'm about to be given my long-awaited culinary accolades for a job well done!" Instead, Cher lectured me on what I already knew—how she would prefer her snow peas in future culinary concoctions: "Andy, from now on I want my snow peas submissive! I want my snow peas the way I want my men—submissive!"

Vegetable Pasta with Low-Fat Pesto Sauce

Pesto sauce: Makes 1 2/3 cups
Pasta and vegetables (with sauce): Serves 4

her loves pasta but doesn't like having an entire meal based solely on carbohydrates. So I developed this recipe, which feels like eating pasta, when in fact it is mostly long strands of julienned vegetables (easily prepared with a mandoline—see "Andy's Equipment List," page 26).

The star of this dish is the low-fat pesto sauce. I have modified this traditionally high-fat mixture based on olive oil and cheese by using a fresh bread base, which binds the pesto but does not add the inordinate amounts of calories and fat. The pesto is then combined with vegetable broth and thickened with cornstarch to produce a velvety smooth sauce. Because of the nature of this low-fat sauce, it is vital that it be prepared close to serving time to maximize its flavor and color.

The sauce can also be used on polenta, vegetables, or chicken.

VEGETABLES (see NOTE):
  3 large carrots, peeled and julienned lengthwise
  4 medium zucchini, stems removed and outermost skin julienned
    lengthwise
  4 to 5 medum yellow summer squash, stems removed and outermost
    skin julienned lengthwise
LOW-FAT PESTO SAUCE:
  2 tablespoons pine nuts
  1/2 cup fresh white bread crumbs
  1 1/4 cups firmly packed fresh basil leaves, tough stems removed (two
    2/3-ounce bags)
  1/4 cup chopped parsley
  2 teaspoons chopped garlic
  1 teaspoon extra-virgin olive oil
  Dash of salt and freshly ground black pepper
  1/4 cup white wine
  1 tablespoon plus 1/2 teaspoon cornstarch
  1 1/4 cups vegetable broth

  1/4 pound angel hair (capellini) or fedellini pasta
  Freshly grated Parmesan or Asiago cheese, to sprinkle over servings
    (optional)

To prepare the vegetables, bring a medium-size pot of salted water to a boil. Add the carrots and cook 1 minute. Immediately add the zucchini and yellow squash and cook an additional 1 to 2 minutes, long enough to soften the vegetables but not so long that they are soggy or falling apart. Drain and refresh under cold running water. Drain thoroughly and set aside. Refill the same pot with salted water and bring to a boil.

To prepare the sauce, in a small skillet, dry-roast the pine nuts over medium heat until golden-brown, about 3 to 4 minutes, shaking the pan to prevent them from burning (dry roasting brings out the oils in the nuts and will add a wonderful nutty flavor to the pesto). Set aside to cool.

In a food processor fitted with a metal blade, or in a blender, combine the bread crumbs, basil, parsley, garlic, olive oil, pine nuts, salt, and black pepper. Process the mixture a few seconds until it becomes a smooth, thick paste. Scrape the sides down with a rubber spatula and add the wine. Process again to incorporate the wine and make the sauce homogeneous.

In a small pot, mix the cornstarch and vegetable broth until smooth. Stirring constantly, bring to a boil over medium heat; boil for 1 minute. Stir in the pesto, then remove from the heat.

Add the pasta to the pot of boiling water and cook to just before it reaches al dente (since thin pasta has a tendency to overcook very quickly), about 3 minutes. Meanwhile, in a wide skillet over medium heat, combine the pesto sauce and vegetables; return it to a boil. When the pasta is done, drain thoroughly and add it to the pesto-vegetable mixture. Mix to thoroughly heat and distribute all the ingredients.

Serve in pasta bowls with the freshly grated cheese, if using, sprinkled over each serving.

NOTE:

There are two reasons why only the outermost skin of the zucchini and yellow squash is used in this recipe. First, it is the color of the vegetable skin that you want to vibrantly show up in this pasta; the inner cores would not show this color. Secondly, the inner cores, if julienned, would break up when cooked, thus defeating the "pastalike" effect. Nevertheless, in an effort to reduce waste, the cores can be diced and used in ratatouille or a simple vegetable sauté.

NUTRITIONAL ANALYSIS PER SERVING (vegetable pasta and sauce—1¾ cups per serving):
Calories: 300 • Protein: 11 grams • Carbohydrates: 52.5 grams • Fiber: 8 grams • Fat: Total: 5 grams • Saturated: 0.5 gram • Cholesterol: 0 • Sodium: 517 milligrams

Vegetable Side Dishes

Grilled Ratatouille

Serves 6

his classic vegetable stew takes on a new dimension of flavor if you grill the vegetables prior to finishing the preparation on the stovetop. The vegetables caramelize on the hot grill and render some of their moisture; the end result is a sweet, smoky vegetable stew that is not watery and doesn't take a long time to cook.

> 1 small eggplant (about ¾ pound), peeled and sliced into
> ½-inch-thick rounds
> 1 tablespoon plus ¼ teaspoon salt
> 1 red bell pepper, halved and seeded
> 1 yellow bell pepper, halved and seeded
> 2 medium zucchini, halved lengthwise
> 4 small yellow summer squash, halved lengthwise
> 8 small whole white mushrooms, scrubbed and rinsed
> 1 large red onion, cut into ¾-inch-thick rounds
> 3 small tomatoes (about 1½ pounds), cored and cut into 1-inch-thick
> rounds
> 2 tablespoons extra-virgin olive oil
> ⅓ cup chopped parsley, plus extra for garnish
> 1 teaspoon garlic salt
> Freshly ground black pepper
> ⅓ cup chopped garlic
> 1½ teaspoons herbes de Provence

Preheat a barbecue grill to medium-hot.

Soak the eggplant rounds in 1½ quarts of lukewarm water with 1 tablespoon of the salt added. This leaches any bitterness out of the eggplant. Set aside.

Meanwhile, place the bell peppers, zucchini, yellow squash, mushrooms, red onion, and tomatoes on a baking sheet or in a large mixing bowl.

Combine 1 tablespoon of the olive oil with the parsley, garlic salt, and black pepper in a small cup. Remove the eggplant from the water, pat dry, and add the eggplant to the other vegetables. Rub the parsley-olive oil mixture over all surfaces of the prepared vegetables.

Using long-handled tongs and a spatula, grill the vegetables until lightly charred and marked by the grill, turning once, about 10 to 15 minutes. Remove from the grill.

Remove the skin from the tomato rounds, chop into 1-inch pieces, and set aside. Chop the remaining vegetables into ³/₄-inch pieces and keep them separate from the tomatoes.

Heat the remaining 1 tablespoon of olive oil in a large pot over medium heat. Add the garlic and sauté a few seconds until fragrant but not browned. Add the chopped vegetables except the tomatoes and sauté 5 to 7 minutes. Add the tomatoes, herbes de Provence, and the remaining ¹/₄ teaspoon of salt. Simmer, uncovered, about 30 minutes, stirring occasionally.

Adjust seasoning, if necessary, with additional herbes de Provence, salt, or freshly ground black pepper. Serve hot or chilled, sprinkled with a little chopped parsley.

NUTRITIONAL ANALYSIS PER SERVING:
Calories: 121 • Protein: 4 grams • Carbohydrates: 18.1 grams • Fiber: 5.5 grams • Fat: Total: 5.23 grams • Saturated: 0.736 gram • Cholesterol: 0 • Sodium: 282 milligrams

Chastity's Italian Spinach and Onions

Makes about 5¹/₂ cups; 6 to 8 servings

I was given this recipe by Chastity Bono and ever since I can always be found the night before Thanksgiving or on Christmas Eve quietly washing the mounds of spinach to make this dish (the calm before the storm!). It is a holiday favorite in Cher's family. This spinach attains an almost creamy consistency from first blanching the leaves in boiling, salted water, which intensifies the color and renders the spinach of some of its moisture, and then slow-cooking it. Chastity likes to use what may seem like a lot of garlic here, but once you try making it, you will understand why it's such a treat.

> 1 tablespoon plus ¹/₄ teaspoon salt, or more
> 4¹/₂ pounds fresh spinach, roots removed and discarded, leaves thoroughly washed (see page 65)
> ¹/₄ cup olive oil
> 2 large onions, chopped
> ¹/₂ cup finely chopped garlic
> ¹/₂ teaspoon freshly ground black pepper

Bring a large pot of water and 1 tablespoon of the salt to a boil. In two or more batches, plunge the spinach into the boiling water and cook until wilted but still bright green, 3 to 4 minutes. Remove with a slotted spoon or tongs and drain well in a colander. Squeeze any excess liquid from the spinach. (Alternatively, to steam the spinach, fit a pot with a steamer insert and a shallow amount of water. Bring the water to a boil, add the spinach, cover the pot, and steam until wilted.) Roughly chop and set aside. Drain, rinse, and dry the pot for the next step.

Heat the olive oil in the pot and sauté the onions over medium heat until slightly browned, about 10 minutes. Add the garlic and sauté another 1 to 2 minutes. Add the chopped spinach and slowly sauté until very soft and most of the juices have cooked off, about 25 minutes, tossing to mix the ingredients. Season with the remaining ¹/₄ teaspoon of salt, or more to taste, and the ground pepper. When done, the spinach will have an almost creamy, satiny consistency and a nutlike taste. Serve either hot or at room temperature.

NUTRITIONAL ANALYSIS PER SERVING:
Calories: 171 • Protein: 4 grams • Carbohydrates: 18.1 grams • Fiber: 5.5 grams • Fat: Total: 5.23 grams • Saturated: 0.736 gram • Cholesterol: 0 • Sodium: 282 milligrams

The Rise, and Fall, of Chastity's Spinach

*T*his could have been an *I Love Lucy* episode. Several years ago, Cher had a new house built. Two nights before Christmas, with the help of contractors, carpenters, landscapers, and decorators, we were furiously readying the house for the holidays. I had just finished setting up the kitchen when Chastity arrived from the airport. She is amazing in the kitchen and loves to cook, so we started planning the holiday meals; her spinach recipe was a must.

The next day, Christmas Eve, I brought back a case of fresh spinach from the market to prepare her family favorite. Chas and I needed to wash the spinach carefully, so we plugged the new sinks and began filling them with water, never expecting what was about to come. Sinks almost full, we dump the fresh spinach in, only to have the entire sink unit fall through the countertop from the weight! The carpenters had not yet fastened the sink to the countertop. We were in hysterics.

Solution-minded as I am, I figure'd that we just needed to drain the water. So I unplugged the drains and a cascade of water poured out onto the kitchen floor! The plumbers had not yet connected the pipes either. Needless to say, Chas and I laughed all the way to the dinner table.

Yellow Summer Squash, Shallots, and Sun-Dried Tomatoes

Makes 6 1/2 cups; 6 to 8 servings

Shallots and sun-dried tomatoes add a pronounced flavor to delicate summer squash in this light side dish. For best results, cook the squash in two batches so it will brown properly and does not become waterlogged in its own juices.

1/4 cup sun-dried tomatoes (not packed in oil)
2 teaspoons butter
2 1/2 pounds yellow summer squash, halved lengthwise and thinly sliced (about 10 cups)
4 ounces shallots, halved and thinly sliced lengthwise (about 3/4 cup)
Salt
Freshly ground black pepper

In a small bowl, cover the sun-dried tomatoes with hot water and allow them to soak about 20 minutes until pliable. (If you need them faster, place the tomatoes in a small pot, cover with water, bring to a boil, remove from the heat, and allow to soak a few minutes.) Drain and slice thin. Set aside.

Melt 1 teaspoon of the butter in a large covered sauté pan. Add half the summer squash and half the shallots. Cover the pan and allow the vegetables to "sweat" (see page 60) for 3 to 4 minutes, or until softened. Stir occasionally. Remove the lid, add salt and pepper to taste, and continue to sauté, over medium heat, a few more minutes until soft and slightly browned. Sprinkle half of the sun-dried tomatoes over the vegetables. Toss, transfer to a bowl, and keep warm.

Repeat with the remaining half of the ingredients, seasoning with salt and pepper to taste. Serve steaming hot.

NUTRITIONAL ANALYSIS PER SERVING:
Calories: 68.5 • Protein: 3.06 grams • Carbohydrates: 12.7 grams • Fiber: 4.00 grams • Fat: Total: 1.76 grams • Saturated: 0.895 gram • Cholesterol: 3.45 milligrams • Sodium: 66.2 milligrams

Cut Grilled Vegetables

Serves 6

If you blanch these vegetables in a microwave or steamer prior to grilling, all of them come out with uniform tenderness. Once grilled and cut, the colorful array of caramelized vegetables makes a striking presentation with almost any meal.

2 medium carrots, peeled (left whole)
1 large red onion, peeled and cut into 3/4-inch-thick rounds
2 medium zucchini, trimmed and halved lengthwise
2 medium yellow summer squash, trimmed and halved lengthwise
2 small Japanese eggplant, trimmed and halved lengthwise
1 red bell pepper, halved and seeded
1 tablespoon extra-virgin olive oil
1 teaspoon garlic salt
1/4 teaspoon freshly ground black pepper
1/3 cup chopped parsley

Preheat a barbecue grill to medium-hot.

On a microwavable plate, arrange the carrots and red onion rounds in a single layer. Loosely cover with plastic wrap. Microwave on high (100%) power for 8 minutes. (Be careful when removing the plate and plastic wrap, as the steam from the accumulated heat may become blisteringly hot after microwaving.) Using a spatula or tongs, place the vegetables on a baking sheet. Microwave the remaining vegetables in the same manner for 4 minutes on high (100%) power. Remove and place these vegetables on the baking sheet. (Alternatively, you may steam the vegetables in a steamer insert until each is almost soft, or offer some resistance when pierced with a knife.)

Combine the olive oil, garlic salt, black pepper, and parsley in a small cup. Rub the vegetables with the parsley–olive oil mixture until well coated.

Using long-handled tongs and a spatula, grill the vegetables until lightly charred and marked by the grill, turning once, about 10 to 15 minutes. Remove and allow to cool slightly.

Cut each vegetable into 3/4-inch chunks and place in a large bowl. Toss to distribute the vegetables evenly. Reheat on the baking sheet or serve at room temperature.

NUTRITIONAL ANALYSIS PER SERVING:
Calories: 70.9 • Protein: 2.49 grams • Carbohydrates: 11.4 grams • Fiber: 3.98 grams • Fat: Total: 2.65 grams • Saturated: 0.381 gram • Cholesterol: 0 • Sodium: 193 milligrams

Grilled Corn and Green Chile Peppers

Makes 8 to 8 1/2 cups; serves 8

Corn on the cob is the perfect vegetable to grill, because as the outside becomes slightly charred, the kernels still remain moist from their milky interior. Here the corn kernels are combined with spicy green chiles, but any overwhelming heat is extinguished with fresh lime juice.

2 teaspoons extra-virgin olive oil
1 teaspoon ground cumin
3 tablespoons chopped cilantro
1/4 teaspoon salt
8 ears fresh yellow corn, shucked
3 fresh Anaheim chiles (about 10 ounces)
1/4 cup fresh lime or lemon juice
Freshly ground black pepper

Preheat a barbecue grill to medium-hot.

Combine the olive oil, cumin, 2 tablespoons of the cilantro, and salt in a small cup. Rub this mixture over the ears of corn.

Using long-handled tongs, place the corn and chiles on the grill. Grill the corn, turning until all sides are generally bright yellow with some kernels blackened. Grill the chiles until all of the skin has blistered and is charred. This will take 10 to 15 minutes.

Place the chiles in a plastic bag to steam for 5 to 10 minutes to facilitate removal of the skin. Meanwhile, cut the corn off the cob by standing each ear on end in a large bowl. Using a sharp knife, cut downward, close to the cob, until all the kernels come off on all sides. Remove the chiles from the bag; peel, seed, and cut into 1/4-inch dice. Add to the bowl containing the cut corn.

To the corn-chile mixture, add the remaining 1 tablespoon of cilantro and the lime juice. Mix thoroughly. Adjust seasoning with salt and pepper to taste. Serve warm.

NUTRITIONAL ANALYSIS PER 1-CUP SERVING:
Calories: 138 • Protein: 4.27 grams • Carbohydrates: 30.4 grams • Fiber: 5.26 grams • Fat: Total: 2.28 grams • Saturated: 0.319 gram • Cholesterol: 0 • Sodium: 590 milligrams

Spinach-Carrot Rolls

Makes 20 individual sushi-size rounds

*magine vegetable sushi, but instead of rice, steamed spin-
ach leaves are the wrapper surrounding bright-orange julienned carrots. This is accomplished by laying the julienned
carrots on a pile of flattened spinach leaves, then rolling the spinach around the
carrots, and steaming the roll just until the spinach is wilted. The roll is then sliced
into sushi-style rounds to reveal the beautiful carrot centers. Excellent served with
Oriental Wontons and Dipping Sauce (page 51) or Crisp Sea Scallops in Spicy
Roasted Red Pepper Sauce (page 87).*

3 pounds fresh spinach (with stems)
5 large carrots, peeled and cut into long julienne strips (the length of
the carrots)
1 teaspoon all-purpose seasoning, such as Spike or Mrs. Dash

Place a large wide pot, fitted with a steamer insert, on the stove. Fill with about
1 inch of water. Bring the water to a boil.

On a cutting board, cut off and discard the bottom 1 inch of the roots from
each bunch of spinach. Fill a sink full of cool water and rinse the spinach in
several changes of water (see page 65). There is no need to dry the spinach. Set
aside.

Spread out the carrots in a thin layer on the steamer insert. Cover the pot
and steam 2 to 3 minutes to soften the carrots. Set aside to cool, leaving the
steamer set up.

On a clean work surface, divide the spinach into 4 equal amounts. One
bunch at a time, line up half the leaves to point in one direction. Lay the other
half on top with the leaves pointing in the opposite direction, with the stems
meeting in the middle (you should end up with a flat pile about 7 to 8 inches
long). Lay 1/4 of the julienned carrot strips down the center of the arranged
spinach leaves. Sprinkle 1/4 teaspoon of the seasoning over the carrots. Starting
from a long side, roll the spinach leaves around the carrots, forming a long
cylindrical roll. Repeat with the remaining spinach bunches and carrots.

Place each roll on the steamer (you may need to do this in 2 batches). Cover
the pot and steam 4 to 5 minutes, or until the spinach has wilted and cooked
through. Using a long spatula, gently remove the rolls, being careful not to let
them fall apart, and set them on the cutting board to cool.

When the rolls are cool enough to handle, squeeze out any excess water from each of them. Trim off any ragged ends, then cut each roll crosswise into 5 equal-size rounds, each about 1½ inches wide.

On a plate (or the steamer tray if reheating), lay the pieces with a cut side up so that you can see the bright carrot center from above. May be served hot or chilled.

NUTRITIONAL ANALYSIS PER SERVING:
Calories: 75.6 • Protein: 7.14 grams • Carbohydrates: 14 grams • Fiber: 7.67 grams • Fat: Total: 0.908 grams • Saturated: 0.145 gram • Cholesterol: 0 • Sodium: 200 milligrams

Carrot-Lemon Purée

Makes 4 cups; serves 6 to 8

A light purée of carrots with the refreshing tartness of lemon zest. The oils in the outer skin of the lemon contain the most concentrated flavor and lend a contrasting flavor to the sweet carrots without the acidity of lemon juice.

3¼ pounds carrots, peeled and cut into ¾-inch pieces (7 cups)
1 cup diced, peeled russet or Idaho potatoes
½ teaspoon salt
1 teaspoon finely chopped lemon zest (see page 47)

In a medium pot, combine the carrots, potatoes, salt, and enough water to cover. Bring to a boil, cover, and cook 20 minutes, or until soft. Drain.

Pour the carrot-potato mixture into a food processor fitted with a metal blade. Add the lemon zest and process several minutes until velvety smooth. (Alternatively, if you do not have a food processor use a hand-held potato masher. It will work just as well, although the consistency may not be as smooth.)

The purée can simply be spooned onto individual plates, or a pastry bag fitted with a decorative tip may be used to pipe out more formal-looking portions.

NOTE:
The purée can be prepared up to 2 days ahead, covered, and refrigerated. About 10 minutes prior to serving, reheat the purée in a covered pot over medium-low heat until hot, stirring occasionally.

NUTRITIONAL ANALYSIS PER SERVING:
Calories: 132 • Protein: 3.1 grams • Carbohydrates: 30.9 grams • Fiber: 6.82 grams • Fat: Total: 0.495 gram • Saturated: 0.086 gram • Cholesterol: 0 • Sodium: 68 milligrams

Crisp Potato Thins

Serves 6 to 8

*T*he French make a potato dish called Pommes Anna, in which thinly sliced potatoes are mixed with huge amounts of melted butter, layered in a pan, and baked, or cooked on the stovetop. They are delicious, but not a good choice for the health- and heart-conscious.

I decided to develop a low-fat version of this dish, made without any butter. The potatoes are thinly sliced and partially cooked in chicken broth, along with sliced onions. The potatoes and onions are then mixed with herbs and seasonings and baked in a very hot oven. The high heat serves to brown the edges of the potatoes quickly while leaving them moist, and also helps to prevent sticking.

> 1 can (14$^1/_2$ ounces) low-sodium chicken broth
> 1 teaspoon salt
> 3$^1/_2$ pounds Idaho potatoes, peeled and cut into thin rounds
> 2 medium onions, halved and cut into $^1/_4$-inch-thick slices
> 2 teaspoons coarsely chopped fresh rosemary
> $^1/_4$ teaspoon freshly ground black pepper
> $^1/_2$ teaspoon garlic salt
> Vegetable oil cooking spray

Preheat the oven to 450 degrees F. Position the shelf in the upper part of the oven.

In a large pot, bring the chicken broth, about 6 cups of water, and the salt to a simmer. The amount of liquid should be approximately double the volume of the potatoes and onions combined.

Add the potatoes and onions to the broth and simmer gently until crisp-tender or parcooked, 10 to 15 minutes. With a slotted spoon, gently move the potatoes and onions around in the broth so they cook evenly. When ready, the potatoes should be pliable, but not so soft that they fall apart. Drain in a colander, discarding the broth, and pour the potato-onion mixture into a large bowl.

Gently toss the potatoes and onions with the rosemary, black pepper, and garlic salt.

Coat a baking sheet with a thin film of vegetable oil cooking spray. Pour the potato-onion mixture onto the baking sheet, spread it out, and lightly spray the tops with more cooking spray. Bake until the potatoes begin to crisp and brown around the edges, about 5 minutes; then, using a spatula, turn the potatoes over and bake 4 to 5 minutes more. (Some ovens may not get hot enough to brown the potatoes quickly. In this event, turn on the broiler and finish browning under the broiler. Watch closely, since the onions may burn quickly.)

Remove the clusters of crisp potatoes and onions from the baking sheet and serve.

NUTRITIONAL ANALYSIS PER SERVING:
Calories: 277 • Protein: 7.22 grams • Carbohydrates: 62 grams • Fiber: 0.74 grams • Fat: Total: 0.74 gram • Saturated: 0.195 grams • Cholesterol: 0 • Sodium: 322 milligrams

Horseradish Mashed Potatoes

Serves 6 to 8

orseradish is a great way to mask the near-absence of butter and still deliver a lot of flavor. I often serve this variation of mashed potatoes with my Beef Stew and Vegetables (page 125) or Chicken Rollatini with Sun-Dried Tomatoes (page 112). The No-Fat Homemade Gravy (page 119) is excellent over these.

3½ pounds Idaho potatoes, peeled and quartered
1¼ teaspoons salt
¾ cup nonfat milk, warmed
2 teaspoons butter
1 teaspoon prepared horseradish, or more
Pinch of ground white pepper

Place the potatoes in a large pot with 1 teaspoon of the salt and cold water to cover. Bring to a boil, reduce the heat, and simmer, covered, until tender but not falling apart, about 30 minutes. Test by piercing the potatoes with a paring knife, which should slide in easily. Gently pour the potatoes into a colander to drain.

Place the potatoes in a large mixing bowl and, using an electric mixer or hand-held potato masher, lightly break them up. Slowly add the milk and mash the potatoes until all of the liquid is absorbed and the potatoes are light and fluffy. Mix in the butter, horseradish, white pepper, and the remaining ¼ teaspoon of salt. Serve piping hot. If you must hold these for any length of time before serving, cover the bowl and place it in the oven at 200 degrees F.

NUTRITIONAL ANALYSIS PER SERVING:
Calories: 268 • Protein: 6.28 grams • Carbohydrates: 58.7 grams • Fiber: 3.99 grams • Fat: Total: 1.60 grams • Saturated: 0.906 gram • Cholesterol: 4 milligrams • Sodium: 132 milligrams

Holiday Spice Whipped Yams

Makes about 6 cups; serves 8

*T*hese velvety, seductively sweet yams are mixed with traditional pie spices and citrus zest to make a light variation of candied yams. This is a holiday favorite in Cher's family, although it is excellent anytime, served with roast turkey, ham, chicken, or pork. When I am busy during the holidays, I usually prepare this dish up to several weeks ahead and freeze it, defrosting the day before heating and serving.

For a more formal occasion, the yam mixture may be placed in a pastry bag fitted with a decorative tip and piped into hollowed-out orange halves. The presentation can be made even more dramatic by serving these bright-orange yams with my Cherry-Lemon Cranberry Sauce (page 48) and Cher's Ambrosia (page 45).

> 6 to 7 large yams (about 5$^{1}/_{2}$ pounds), scrubbed
> $^{1}/_{4}$ teaspoon cinnamon
> $^{1}/_{4}$ teaspoon nutmeg
> $^{1}/_{4}$ teaspoon orange zest or lemon zest (see page 47)
> 1 cup evaporated skim milk

Preheat the oven to 375 degrees F.

Place the yams in the oven and bake until soft and easily pierced with a fork, about 1 hour. (This may take more or less time, depending on their size.) Allow the yams to cool enough to handle. Peel and place in a large bowl.

Using an electric mixer or a hand-held potato masher and a stiff whisk, mash the potatoes, then whip at high speed to achieve a smooth consistency. Add the cinnamon, nutmeg, citrus zest, and evaporated milk. Mix well to combine thoroughly. Spoon the mixture into a baking dish large enough to hold the yams. Cover with aluminum foil. (At this point, if this dish is being made in advance, it can be tightly covered and refrigerated for up to 3 days or frozen for several weeks and thawed in the refrigerator 24 hours prior to serving.)

Bake the yams, covered, in a preheated oven at 350 degrees F. until heated through, about 25 minutes.

NUTRITIONAL ANALYSIS PER SERVING:
Calories: 346 • Protein: 7.8 grams • Carbohydrates: 79.4 grams • Fiber: 9.36 grams • Fat: Total: 0.407 gram • Saturated: 0.126 gram • Cholesterol: 1.15 milligrams • Sodium: 67.8 milligrams

Grains and Legumes

Georgia's Corn Bread Dressing

Makes about 7 1/2 cups; serves 6 to 8

have prepared this family recipe year after year during the holidays. Cher's mother, Georgia, insists that the secret to this dressing is using stone-ground cornmeal and baking the corn bread in a cast-iron skillet. It always accompanies Cher's Thanksgiving turkey.

Vegetable oil cooking spray

CORN BREAD:
3/4 cup flour
1 tablespoon baking powder
2 teaspoons sugar
3/4 teaspoon salt
1 1/4 cups stone-ground yellow cornmeal (found in health food sections of most grocery stores or in natural food stores)
1/4 teaspoon poultry seasoning
1 egg
1 cup low-sodium chicken broth
1/3 cup (2/3 stick) unsalted butter, melted

DRESSING:
1 tablespoon butter
3 1/4 cups chopped onions
1 1/2 cups chopped celery
2 teaspoons dried rubbed sage
1/4 teaspoon poultry seasoning
1/2 teaspoon Beau Monde seasoning
1/3 cup chopped parsley
1 can (14 1/2 ounces) low-sodium chicken broth

Preheat the oven to 400 degrees F. and position the shelf in the center of the oven. Lightly coat an 8- or 10-inch cast-iron skillet or 8 x 8 x 2-inch glass baking dish with a thin film of the vegetable oil cooking spray.

To prepare the corn bread: Sift together the flour, baking powder, sugar, and salt in a large bowl. Stir in the cornmeal and poultry seasoning.

In a small bowl, beat the egg lightly and whisk in the chicken broth and melted butter.

Lightly stir the egg mixture into the dry ingredients. Pour the batter into the prepared skillet and bake for 20 to 25 minutes, until light golden brown. Allow to cool enough to handle, then crumble into a large bowl. Reduce the oven temperature to 350 degrees F.

To prepare the dressing ingredients: In a large sauté pan, melt the butter and sauté the onions and celery until soft, about 8 to 10 minutes. To the bowl of crumbled corn bread, add the sautéed onion mixture, sage, poultry seasoning, Beau Monde seasoning, and parsley. Mix well. Slowly add the chicken broth while mixing until evenly distributed. (At this point the dressing can be spooned into a turkey, if you are roasting a turkey.)

Using the vegetable oil cooking spray, lightly coat a baking dish large enough to hold the dressing. Spoon the dressing into the dish, cover with aluminum foil, and bake at 350 degrees F. for about 45 minutes. Remove the foil, stir up the crispy bottom, add more liquid (water or chicken broth) if the dressing seems dry, and continue to bake until slightly browned and crisp on top, about 15 to 20 minutes more. Serve hot alongside carved roasted turkey or chicken.

NUTRITIONAL ANALYSIS PER SERVING:
Calories: 325 • Protein: 7.53 grams • Carbohydrates: 42.8 grams • Fiber: 4.63 grams • Fat: Total: 15 grams • Saturated: 8.44 grams • Cholesterol: 70 milligrams • Sodium: 732 milligrams

Cher and Her ''French Chef''

One of the funniest moments of my cooking career came as a result of a tabloid article a week after Cher, about twelve house guests, and I gathered in Aspen one year to celebrate the holidays. While I was preparing festive holiday fare, Cher and one of her guests decided to dare the Aspen crowds (and paparazzi) for some last-minute Christmas shopping.

The very next week, a tabloid published a picture of Cher and her friend, headlining her "newfound love in the romantic snow-covered peaks of Colorado." The best came when the article went on to describe the two having prebreakfast trysts and cuddling at romantic candlelight dinners prepared by "her private French chef." Me, a French chef? Ah, what fun it is to be a tabloid character! I can't describe how wonderfully romantic and intimate a holiday meal is, at a table of twelve.

Mexican Corn Bread

Makes 9 to 12 cut slices or 12 muffins

*T*he appeal of this corn bread stems from the sweetness of fresh corn and buttermilk, with an added zip from roasted green chiles. It can be made in a large pan or as individual muffins, and is a perfect addition to nearly any meal. If it is baked in a cast-iron skillet, the corn bread's sugar will caramelize, creating an extra-crispy exterior crust that contrasts with the delicate, moist interior.

1 cup all-purpose flour or bread flour
$^1/_4$ cup sugar
1 tablespoon baking powder
1 teaspoon salt
1 cup yellow cornmeal
1 extra-large egg, lightly beaten
$^1/_3$ cup safflower oil or melted butter
$1^1/_4$ cups low-fat buttermilk
1 cup frozen corn kernels, thawed
1 can (7 ounces) diced mild green chiles, 2 tablespoons reserved for
  garnishing

Preheat the oven to 425 degrees F. Lightly coat an 8 x 8 x 2-inch baking dish, a 9-inch round baking pan, a 10-inch cast-iron skillet, or 12 foil cup liners (placed in a muffin tin) with a thin film of vegetable oil cooking spray.

In a large bowl, sift together the flour, sugar, baking powder, and salt. Stir in the cornmeal.

In a small bowl, whisk together the egg, oil, and buttermilk.

Lightly stir the egg mixture into the dry ingredients. The batter will be lumpy. Be careful not to overwork the batter, as that will produce tough corn bread. Gently fold in the corn kernels and all but the 2 tablespoons of green chiles and stir until just mixed.

Pour the batter into the prepared pan or almost fill the muffin cups. Garnish the top of the batter with the reserved green chiles and bake for about 25 minutes, or until light golden brown on top. Serve warm or at room temperature, cutting the bread into individual slices.

Nutritional Analysis per Serving:
Calories: 246 • Protein: 5.76 grams • Carbohydrates: 35.4 grams • Fiber: 2.70 grams • Fat: Total: 9.48 grams • Saturated: 1.18 grams • Cholesterol: 24.7 milligrams • Sodium: 465 milligrams

Vibrant Verde Rice

Serves 8

*D*elicious with many Mexican meals, this rice is cooked with a purée of fresh parsley, cilantro, and roasted green chiles, preferably poblanos. The purée, added at the beginning of cooking the rice, gives it a vibrant geen color and distinct chile flavor without being overwhelmingly spicy.

> 3 fresh poblano or other mild green chiles (about 1/2 pound), roasted, peeled, and seeded (see page 157)
> 3/4 cup chopped parsley
> 3/4 cup chopped cilantro
> 3 cloves garlic, peeled
> 2 teaspoons extra-virgin olive oil
> 2 medium onions, finely chopped
> 2 1/2 cups raw white rice
> 1/2 teaspoon ground cumin or cumin seed
> 5 cups low-sodium chicken broth or water
> 1/2 teaspoon salt

In a food processor fitted with a metal blade, purée the chiles, parsley, cilantro, and garlic cloves. Reserve.

In a wide pot, heat the olive oil and sauté the onions over medium heat until softened, 5 to 7 minutes. Add the rice, cumin, and green chile purée. Stir to coat the rice. Add the chicken broth and salt.

Bring the mixture to a boil, then reduce the heat to low. Cover the pot and simmer slowly until all the liquid is absorbed, 15 to 18 minutes. Remove from the heat and let stand, covered, 5 to 10 minutes more. Fluff the rice with a fork. Serve hot.

NUTRITIONAL ANALYSIS PER SERVING:
Calories: 263 • Protein: 6.96 grams • Carbohydrates: 52.5 grams • Fiber: 2.87 grams • Fat: Total: 3.06 grams • Saturated: 0.925 grams • Cholesterol: 3.12 milligrams • Sodium: 625 milligrams

Lemon-Dill Rice

Makes about 8 cups; serves 6 to 8

This is a wonderful side dish with a light, summery citrus flavor.

2 teaspoons extra-virgin olive oil
1 large onion, chopped
2 cups raw white rice
1 tablespoon lemon zest (see page 47)
$^{1}/_{3}$ to $^{1}/_{2}$ cup fresh lemon juice
Pinch of crushed dried oregano
$^{1}/_{4}$ cup snipped fresh dill
$^{3}/_{4}$ teaspoon salt

In a medium-size saucepan, heat the olive oil and sauté the onions over medium heat until translucent but not turning brown, about 5 minutes. Add the rice and stir to coat. Add the lemon zest, lemon juice, 4 cups of water, the oregano, dill, and salt.

Bring to a boil, then reduce the heat to the lowest setting. Cover the pot and simmer slowly until all the liquid is absorbed, about 20 minutes. Remove from the heat and let stand, covered, 5 to 10 minutes more. Fluff the rice with a fork and serve.

VARIATIONS AND SUGGESTIONS:
For a dramatic presentation, try stuffing steamed artichokes with this rice. On hot summer days, stuff the artichokes earlier in the day and chill them until ready to serve. Garnish with thinly sliced lemon rounds and fresh dill sprigs.

NUTRITIONAL ANALYSIS PER SERVING:
Calories: 256 • Protein: 4.58 grams • Carbohydrates: 54.0 grams • Fiber: 1.66 grams • Fat: Total: 1.91 grams • Saturated: 0.308 gram • Cholesterol: 0 • Sodium: 271 milligrams

Chutney Basmati Rice

Serves 8 to 10

*D*elicious as an accompaniment to grilled eggplant, vegetable stews, and many Indian meals, such as curry or tandoori meats.

2 teaspoons butter
2¹/₂ cups chopped onions
¹/₂ teaspoon curry powder (optional)
2¹/₂ cups raw basmati rice
3 tablespoons finely chopped mango chutney (found in the condiment section of most grocery stores; I like Major Grey's)
1 tablespoon currants or golden raisins
¹/₂ teaspoon salt
¹/₄ cup toasted pine nuts

Melt the butter in a 5-quart saucepan and sauté the onions over medium heat until translucent but not turning brown, about 5 minutes. Stir in the curry powder, if using, and cook a few seconds until fragrant. Add the rice and stir to coat thoroughly. Add the mango chutney, 4 cups of water, the currants, and salt. Bring to a boil, then reduce the heat to the lowest setting. Cover the pot and simmer slowly until all the liquid is absorbed, about 15 minutes. Remove from the heat and let stand, covered, 5 to 10 minutes more.

Fluff the rice with a fork and stir in the pine nuts. Serve hot.

NUTRITIONAL ANALYSIS PER SERVING:
Calories: 180 • Protein: 4.28 grams • Carbohydrates: 33.2 grams • Fiber: 1.80 grams • Fat: Total: 3.86 grams • Saturated: 1.05 grams • Cholesterol: 2.59 milligrams • Sodium: 161 milligrams

Oriental Fried Rice

Makes about 7 to 8 cups; serves 6 to 8

A traditional combination of rice, vegetables, and eggs, lightly stir-fried and served steaming hot. I use brown rice to achieve more of a "fried" visual effect, since such a small amount of oil is used. A nonstick sauté pan or wok works best to prevent the rice from sticking to the pan. This is an excellent accompaniment to Oriental Wontons and Dipping Sauce (page 51), Grilled Tuna and Papaya-Mint Salsa (page 82), or as a vegetarian meal with the addition of some cubed tofu.

1 teaspoon peanut or vegetable oil
$1/4$ teaspoon dark sesame oil
3 medium carrots, cut into short julienne pieces
2 stalks celery, thinly sliced
1 cup bean sprouts
2 cups raw brown rice, cooked according to package directions and
  allowed to cool
1 teaspoon low-sodium soy sauce, or more
2 whole eggs or 4 egg whites, partially scrambled
4 green onions, thinly sliced, plus extra for garnish
$1/2$ cup frozen green peas, thawed

Depending upon the size of the pan or wok you use, it will probably be necessary to fry the rice in 2 or 3 batches. Therefore, divide all of the ingredients accordingly and proceed with the following instructions.

In a large nonstick sauté pan or wok, heat the peanut oil and sesame oil over high heat. Add the carrots, celery, and bean sprouts and lightly brown, 6 to 8 minutes. Stir in the rice and continue cooking 2 to 3 minutes. Mix in the soy sauce.

Make a well in the center of the rice and add the eggs. Allow the eggs to set slightly before stirring them into the surrounding rice. Mix in the green onions and peas and cook just long enough to heat through. Adjust seasoning with more soy sauce, if needed. Serve with additional green onions sprinkled over the top.

NUTRITIONAL ANALYSIS PER SERVING:
Calories: 298 • Protein: 8.87 grams • Carbohydrates: 55.4 grams • Fiber: 4.48 grams • Fat: Total: 4.68 grams • Saturated: 1.09 grams • Cholesterol: 70.7 milligrams • Sodium: 90.8 milligrams

Fat-Free Black Beans with Lime and Jalapeño Chiles

*Makes about 6 to 7 cups;
serves 6 to 10 as a side dish*

Black beans, also known as turtle beans, take on a lighter, tropical flavor with the addition of lime and the subtle but not overwhelming heat from fresh jalapeño chiles. They are prepared in the spirit of refried beans—half the cooked beans are puréed, to achieve a similar texture. If you prefer soupier whole beans, don't purée them. Also, the skins of beans toughen if salt is added early in the cooking, so add the salt toward the end of the cooking process to ensure tender beans.

1 pound (about 2 cups) dried black beans, picked over and rinsed
1³/₄ cups chopped onions
3 to 4 cloves garlic, peeled
2 medium fresh jalapeño chiles, seeded and minced
¹/₄ cup chopped cilantro
¹/₄ teaspoon ground cumin
1 teaspoon salt
¹/₂ teaspoon finely chopped lime zest (see page 47)
1¹/₂ tablespoons fresh lime juice
Thin slices of lime, for garnish

Put the beans and just enough water to cover them in a medium pot. Bring to a boil and immediately drain the beans into a colander, discarding the water. Rinse the pot.

Return the beans to the same pot and add the onions, garlic, jalapeños, cilantro, and cumin. Cover with 9 cups of water. Bring to a boil and then reduce the heat to low. Cover the pot, simmer 1 hour, and then add the salt. Continue to simmer, covered, until the beans are tender, 15 to 25 minutes more.

Purée half the beans and their cooking liquid in a food processor fitted with a metal blade, or in batches in a blender. Return the puréed beans to the pot and mix in the lime zest and lime juice. Stir until fully incorporated, then taste and adjust seasoning, if necessary. (The beans may be prepared to this point up to 3 days in advance, covered, and refrigerated, or frozen for up to 2 months.) Reheat before serving.

Garnish each serving of beans with a thin sliver of lime.

NUTRITIONAL ANALYSIS PER SERVING:
Calories: 174 • Protein: 10.9 grams • Carbohydrates: 32.4 grams • Fiber: 11 grams • Fat: Total: 0.744 gram • Saturated: 0.177 gram • Cholesterol: 0 • Sodium: 441 milligrams

Unfried Refried Beans

Makes about 6 to 7 cups;
serves 8 to 10 as a side dish

Cher loves to have these silky smooth, fat-free pinto beans with enchiladas, burritos, or other Mexican-inspired meals. They may be prepared up to 3 days in advance, and I usually make extra because they freeze well and can be added to burritos for quick snacks or meals. Arriba!

1 pound (about 2¹/₄ cups) dried pinto beans, picked over and rinsed
3 cups chopped onions
1 teaspoon ground cumin
¹/₂ teaspoon chili powder
1 teaspoon chopped cilantro
1 teaspoon salt
Grated low-fat Cheddar or Jack cheese (optional)
Low-fat sour cream (optional)

Put the beans and just enough water to cover them in a medium pot. Bring to a boil and immediately drain the beans into a colander, discarding the water. Rinse the pot.

Return the beans to the same pot and add the onions, cumin, chili powder, and cilantro. Cover with 7 cups of water. Bring to a boil and then reduce the heat to low. Cover the pot, simmer 1¹/₂ hours, and then add the salt. Continue to simmer, covered, until the beans are tender, about 30 minutes more.

Purée all the beans with their cooking liquid in a food processor fitted with a metal blade, or in batches in a blender. The purée should resemble a thick paste, but if it is too thick, the consistency may be adjusted by adding more water. (Depending on the capacity of your machine, you may need to do this in several batches.) Taste the beans and adjust the seasoning, if needed, with additional salt or ground cumin. (The beans may be prepared to this point up to 3 days in advance, covered, and refrigerated, or frozen for up to 2 months.) Reheat to serve.

Serve in small bowls. Garnish with a sprinkling of the optional grated cheese, melted under your oven broiler for a few seconds, and add a dollop of sour cream if you like.

NUTRITIONAL ANALYSIS PER SERVING (without garnish):
Calories: 154 • Protein: 8.63 grams • Carbohydrates: 29.9 grams • Fiber: 9.28 grams • Fat: Total: 0.596 gram • Saturated: 0.12 gram • Cholesterol: 0 • Sodium: 270 milligrams

Cher's BBQ Baked Beans

Serves 8 to 12

Thick-sauced sweet baked beans with a heady barbecue aroma make a winning combination that will bring the neighbors running to your next summer cookout. The beans would nicely complement the Dill Coleslaw (page 42), Grilled Corn and Green Chile Peppers (page 157), and Fajita Skirt Steak (page 129), among other dishes on any garden table.

2 cans (28 ounces each) baked beans
2 tablespoons Dijon mustard
2 tablespoons brown sugar
1/4 cup barbecue sauce, preferably Woody's Cook-in sauce barbecue
   concentrate
2 tablespoons ketchup
1 cup chopped onions

Preheat the oven to 350 degrees F.

Combine all of the ingredients in an ovenproof pot. Cover the pot and bake for 45 minutes, stirring occasionally. (The beans can be prepared up to 3 days ahead, to this point, covered, and refrigerated.) Uncover the pot and continue to cook another 15 to 20 minutes, or until the beans are thick and bubbly. Serve hot or at room temperature.

NUTRITIONAL ANALYSIS PER SERVING (based on 8 servings per recipe):
Calories: 215 • Protein: 10.2 grams • Carbohydrates: 47 grams • Fiber: 10.5 grams • Fat: Total: 1.42 grams • Saturated: 0.274 gram • Cholesterol: 0 • Sodium: 993 milligrams

Desserts

Chocolate, Black Pepper, and Cherry Soufflé

Makes 6 individual soufflés

*M*aybe Cher had it right when she made chocolate her favorite heavenly food, because chocolate comes from the cocoa bean, Theobroma, *meaning "food of the gods." After I first made chocolate soufflés for one of Cher's dinner parties, she suggested that I develop a similar recipe to include other favorite ingredients of hers: black pepper and cherries. This truly has become Cher's trademark dessert!*

Vegetable oil cooking spray
³/₄ cup sugar, plus extra for coating soufflé cups
¹/₂ cup dried cherries
2 tablespoons fresh orange juice
1 teaspoon orange zest (see page 47)
1 tablespoon orange liqueur
1 teaspoon coarse freshly ground black pepper
2 tablespoons cornstarch
1 cup evaporated skim milk
¹/₄ cup cocoa powder
1 teaspoon instant freeze-dried coffee granules
1 egg yolk, slightly beaten
5 egg whites
¹/₂ teaspoon cream of tartar
Confectioners' sugar, for garnish
Softly whipped cream (optional)

Preheat the oven to 375 degrees F. Prepare six 6-ounce soufflé cups by coating them with a thin film of vegetable oil cooking spray and then sprinkling enough sugar into each to coat the bottom and sides thoroughly. Empty out any excess sugar.

To plump the cherries, combine the dried cherries, orange juice, orange zest, and liqueur in a small saucepan over low heat. Gently simmer the mixture until the liquid is gone, 5 to 10 minutes. Remove from the heat and cool. Coarsely chop the plumped cherries and place them in a small cup. Mix in the black pepper. Set aside.

In the same small saucepan, stir together the cornstarch, evaporated milk, ¹/₂ cup of the sugar, the cocoa powder, and instant coffee. Cook over medium heat, stirring constantly, until the chocolate mixture thickens. Remove from the heat and cool slightly. Place the egg yolk in a small cup and add a small amount of the chocolate mixture, whisking constantly, to temper or warm the egg yolk. Pour the egg mixture into the chocolate mixture and whisk thoroughly until fully incorporated. Mix in the cherry–black pepper mixture.

In a mixing bowl, beat the egg whites until foamy. Add the cream of tartar and continue to beat the mixture while slowly adding the remaining 1/4 cup of sugar. Beat the egg whites until soft peaks form.

With a rubber spatula, fold 1/4 of the whites into the chocolate-cherry mixture to lighten the consistency, then gently fold the chocolate mixture into the remaining beaten whites, just until evenly incorporated. Fill each of the prepared ramekins with equal amounts of the soufflé filling, place on a baking sheet, and bake for 20 minutes, until the soufflés have risen. (Keep the oven door closed during baking for the most even heat and to prevent the soufflés from falling.)

Serve them immediately, dusted with a light sprinkling of confectioners' sugar. Pass the whipped cream, if using, in a separate bowl at the table. (Your guests may poke a hole in the soufflé center with a spoon and fill the crater with the whipped cream.)

NUTRITIONAL ANALYSIS PER SERVING:
Calories: 211 • Protein: 7.63 grams • Carbohydrates: 45.6 grams • Fiber: 1.76 grams • Fat: Total: 1.50 grams • Saturated: 0.610 gram • Cholesterol: 37.0 milligrams • Sodium: 144 milligrams

Chocolate Fudge Torte

Serves 12

A rich chocolate dessert that gets its moistness from puréed prunes. Like Cher, any weight-conscious chocolate lover will be thoroughly satisfied by the bittersweet, ultrafudge consistency of this torte.

Vegetable oil cooking spray
1 teaspoon instant freeze-dried espresso granules
$^1/_2$ cup pitted prunes
$^3/_4$ cup evaporated skim milk
$1^1/_4$ cups cocoa powder
$1^1/_4$ cups plus 2 tablespoons sugar
3 tablespoons flour
1 large whole egg, at room temperature
1 large egg yolk, at room temperature
1 teaspoon vanilla extract
2 large egg whites
$^1/_8$ teaspoon cream of tartar
Vanilla frozen yogurt

Preheat the oven to 350 degrees F. Coat the interior sides of an 8 x 2-inch round springform cake pan with a thin film of vegetable oil cooking spray. Using the pan as a guide, trace a round circle on the baking parchment paper. Cut out the circle and line the bottom of the pan with the parchment.

In a small cup, dissolve the espresso granules in 2 teaspoons hot water. In a food processor fitted with a metal blade, or in a blender, purée the prunes and, with the machine running, slowly add the coffee mixture and evaporated milk through the feed tube. Process until smooth. Reserve.

In a heavy medium saucepan, combine the cocoa powder with $1^1/_4$ cups of the sugar and the flour. Add the prune mixture and stir just until the dry ingredients are moistened. (The mixture will be very thick, but do not worry; it will combine.) Heat the mixture over low heat until it begins to thin ever so slightly and the sugar is completely dissolved, 2 to 3 minutes. The chocolate mixture will be glossy and smooth. Remove from the heat and allow to cool slightly.

In a small bowl, lightly beat the egg, egg yolk, and vanilla. When the chocolate mixture is relatively cool, whisk in the egg mixture. Set aside.

Using an electric mixer, beat the egg whites at medium speed until foamy. Add the cream of tartar and beat until soft peaks form when the beaters are lifted from the bowl. Gradually beat in the remaining 2 tablespoons of sugar. Increase the speed to high and beat the whites until stiff but not dry.

Using a rubber spatula, fold one-quarter of the egg whites into the chocolate mixture. Gently fold in the remaining whites.

Pour the batter into the prepared cake pan and smooth the top, if necessary. (Don't worry if you think there's not enough batter; the cake should only be about 1 inch thick). Set the cake pan in a larger baking pan and place in the lower half of the oven. Pour boiling water into the empty baking pan to reach halfway up the sides of the cake pan. Bake for 30 minutes, until the cake springs back when lightly pressed. Remove the cake pan from the water bath and set aside on a wire rack to cool. Wrap the cake (in its pan) in plastic wrap and refrigerate overnight or for up to 2 days.

To serve, release the sides of the springform pan, running a knife around the edges to loosen the cake, if necessary. The torte will be very dense and sticky, so dip a sharp knife into hot water before cutting each slice. Just before serving each slice, remove any parchment that may adhere to the bottom. Serve each slice on a small plate accompanied by a scoop of vanilla frozen yogurt.

NUTRITIONAL ANALYSIS PER SERVING (including ½ cup vanilla frozen yogurt): Calories: 271 • Protein: 7.55 grams • Carbohydrates: 52.4 grams • Fiber: 3.59 grams • Fat: Total: 6.2 grams • Saturated: 3.49 grams • Cholesterol: 37.3 milligrams • Sodium: 109 milligrams

Chocolate Brownies

Makes 15 brownies

These no-guilt brownies with less than half the fat of regular brownies are sure to satisfy the chocolate lover in you. Whenever I bake these brownies, the sweet chocolate aroma that wafts throughout the house always guarantees a big crowd in the kitchen. Their rich flavor comes from good-quality Dutch-process cocoa and moist brown sugar, while applesauce gives them their moist, fudgy consistency.

Butter-flavored vegetable oil cooking spray
1 cup flour
1/2 cup unsweetened cocoa powder, preferably Dutch process
1/2 teaspoon salt
1/4 teaspoon baking powder
1 1/4 cups light brown sugar
3 tablespoons vegetable oil, preferably canola or safflower oil
1 large egg
1 large egg white
2 teaspoons vanilla extract
1/3 cup unsweetened applesauce

Preheat the oven to 350 degrees F. Coat the inside of a 2-quart, 8 x 11 x 2-inch glass baking dish with a thin film of butter-flavored vegetable oil cooking spray. In a small mixing bowl, whisk together the flour, cocoa powder, salt, and baking powder.

In a large bowl, combine the brown sugar, oil, egg, egg white, vanilla, and applesauce. Using an electric mixer, beat on high speed until smooth, making sure no lumps of brown sugar remain. Add the dry ingredients and beat on low speed just until combined. Do not overmix or the brownies will be tough.

Spread the batter in the prepared baking dish. Bake for about 25 minutes, or until a toothpick inserted in the center comes out clean. Let the brownies cool, then cut into 15 squares. Store at room temperature in an airtight container.

VARIATIONS AND SUGGESTIONS:
For a slightly more indulgent treat, you can use these brownies to make wonderful ice-cream sandwiches. Slice each square horizontally to get a top slice and a bottom from each. Place a few spoonfuls of frozen yogurt or ice cream (mint-chocolate chip makes a nice ending to a dinner) on the bottom slice. Cover with

the top slice and lightly press down to form the "sandwich." Eat immediately or wrap in plastic wrap and freeze for later use.

NUTRITIONAL ANALYSIS per brownie:
Calories: 115 • Protein: 2 grams • Carbohydrates: 20.5 grams • Fiber: 1.3 grams • Fat: Total: 3.5 grams • Saturated: 0.5 gram • Cholesterol: 14 milligrams • Sodium: 96 milligrams

Banana–Chocolate Chip Muffins

Makes 12 muffins

*I*t seems I always have a few bananas in the kitchen that are just a little too ripe, so I came up with this incredibly easy, low-fat muffin recipe perfect for morning coffee or a between-meals snack. Bananas and buttermilk lend a delightful moistness to these muffins. If you prefer, bake the batter in a 5¼ x 9 x 2¾-inch loaf pan. Bake the loaf an additional 30 minutes, and slice it when completely cool.

Vegetable oil cooking spray
3 medium-size very ripe bananas (4 if small), peeled
1 egg
⅓ cup low-fat buttermilk or low-fat milk
½ cup granulated sugar
½ cup brown sugar
1½ cups flour
1 teaspoon baking soda
1 teaspoon salt
2 tablespoons chocolate chips
2 tablespoons chopped walnuts (optional)

Preheat the oven to 350 degrees F. Lightly coat 12 foil cup liners with a thin film of the vegetable oil cooking spray. Place them in a muffin tin.

In a large bowl, mash the bananas with a fork. Whisk in the egg, buttermilk, granulated sugar, and brown sugar.

In a separate bowl, combine the flour, baking soda, and salt. Mix together. Add the flour mixture to the banana mixture and combine thoroughly. Fold in the chocolate chips and, if using, the walnuts.

Spoon equal amounts of batter into each of the prepared foil muffin cups. Bake for 30 minutes until browned, or when a toothpick or skewer inserted into the center comes out clean. Allow to cool slightly before serving.

NUTRITIONAL ANALYSIS PER SERVING:
Calories: 131 • Protein: 3.05 grams • Carbohydrates: 26.1 grams • Fiber: 3.59 grams • Fat: Total: 2.06 grams • Saturated: 0.608 gram • Cholesterol: 17.9 milligrams • Sodium: 298 milligrams

Pumpkin Flan

Makes twelve ¹/₂-cup servings

*I*n Cher's home, we call this "pumpkin pie." It tastes just like pumpkin pie without the fattening crust and is a popular snack to have on hand in the refrigerator whenever that sweet tooth needs satisfying.

2 extra-large eggs
2 extra-large egg whites
2 cups nonfat or skim milk
1 can (12 ounces) evaporated low-fat milk
1 can (16 ounces) pumpkin purée
¹/₃ cup sugar
2 teaspoons vanilla extract
2 teaspoons maple extract
¹/₂ teaspoon ground cinnamon, plus extra for sprinkling on top
¹/₄ teaspoon ground nutmeg or freshly grated nutmeg
¹/₈ teaspoon allspice
¹/₄ teaspoon powdered ginger
¹/₄ teaspoon ground mace (optional)
¹/₄ teaspoon salt

Preheat the oven to 325 degrees F. Set out twelve 5-ounce ceramic ramekins or twelve 6-ounce glass custard cups.

In a large mixing bowl, lightly whisk the eggs and egg whites. Add the remaining ingredients to the bowl. Whisk to fully combine all of the ingredients.

Using a ladle or measuring cup with a spout, pour the custard into each of the ramekins, dividing the mixture evenly. Sprinkle a dusting of cinnamon over each filled ramekin.

Arrange the ramekins in a baking dish or roasting pan large enough to hold them without touching. Pour hot tap water into the larger dish to reach halfway up the sides of the ramekins.

Set the baking dish in the lower third of the oven. Bake for approximately 50 to 55 minutes, until the custards are just set. They are done when the centers jiggle slightly when shaken and a cake tester or paring knife inserted into the center comes out clean.

Transfer the ramekins to a rack to cool. When they are cool, cover with plastic wrap and refrigerate until well chilled. Serve chilled or hold in the refrigerator for snacking anytime.

NUTRITIONAL ANALYSIS PER SERVING:
Calories: 90.2 • Protein: 5.55 grams • Carbohydrates: 13.9 grams • Fiber: 1.06 grams • Fat: Total: 1.62 grams • Saturated: 0.72 gram • Cholesterol: 38.4 milligrams • Sodium: 127 milligrams

Nectarine-Blueberry Cobbler

Serves 8

*F*or years I have been making cobblers at the height of the summer fruit season. A cobbler is essentially a pie baked without a fattening, bottom crust. I sprinkle a sweet, crumbly streusel-like crust over the top.

Some summers, Cher has me baking cobblers almost every other day for her and her guests. Everyone seems to love this one, whether for breakfast, to top off a light lunch, or for a perfect ending to a warm summer night.

Any combination of fresh fruits works well in this recipe. Try pairing peaches with black cherries, apricots and blackberries, or raspberries and blackberries. Whatever combination you choose, you can have your cobbler and eat it with a clear conscience too!

Butter-flavored vegetable oil cooking spray
4 pounds ripe nectarines or peaches, peeled, pitted, and cut into large
    slices (about 4 cups)
2 cups blueberries, rinsed and drained
1 tablespoon fresh lemon juice
1 cup plus 2 tablespoons all-purpose flour
3/4 cup granulated sugar
1/2 teaspoon salt
1/2 teaspoon baking powder
1/2 teaspoon baking soda
1/4 teaspoon ground ginger, plus extra for sprinkling on top
2 egg whites, lightly beaten
1 tablespoon melted butter
Low-fat frozen vanilla yogurt

Preheat the oven to 350 degrees F. Position the oven shelf in the center of the oven. Coat the inside of a 2- to 2 1/2-quart casserole with a thin film of butter-flavored vegetable oil cooking spray.

In a bowl, combine the nectarines, blueberries, lemon juice, and 2 tablespoons of the flour. Mix well. Pour the fruit mixture into the casserole and spread the fruit evenly.

In another mixing bowl, combine the remaining 1 cup of flour with the sugar, salt, baking powder, baking soda, and ground ginger. Mix well with a fork. Gradually add the egg whites, stirring with the fork, until the mixture is crumbly. Sprinkle the streusel over the fruit. Drizzle the melted butter over the topping.

Place the cobbler in the oven and bake until golden brown and bubbly, about 35 minutes. Serve hot, warm, or cool, spooned into bowls and topped with the vanilla frozen yogurt. Sprinkle extra ground ginger over the dessert, if desired.

NUTRITIONAL ANALYSIS PER SERVING (including 1 scoop of vanilla low-fat frozen yogurt): Calories: 386 • Protein: 7.42 grams • Carbohydrates: 80.2 grams • Fiber: 5.66 grams • Fat: Total: 5.98 grams • Saturated: 3.43 grams • Cholesterol: 5.32 milligrams • Sodium: 349 milligrams

Grapefruit-Campari Granita

Makes about 7 1/2 to 8 cups; serves 6 as dessert,
12 as a palate refresher

*G*ranita *is a granular ice mixture that is often served between courses to cleanse the palate and stimulate the appetite. Refreshing grapefruit combines with the Italian apéritif Campari to make this a delightful respite either between courses or for dessert. The blush pink ice is especially beautiful if it is presented in martini glasses.*

> 1/2 cup sugar
> 1 quart (32 ounces) strained unsweetened pink grapefruit juice
> 1/2 cup Campari
> 6 fresh mint sprigs, for garnish

Prepare a simple syrup by combining the sugar with 1/4 cup of water in a small saucepan. Place the pan over medium heat and stir until the sugar has dissolved and the liquid is clear, about 5 minutes. Remove from the heat and cool.

In a large bowl, combine the simple syrup mixture with the pink grapefruit juice and Campari. Pour the liquid into an 11 x 7 x 2-inch rectangular glass baking dish and freeze, stirring and crushing lumps with a fork every hour, until the mixture is firm but not frozen solid, about 3 to 4 hours. (The granita may be prepared to this point up to 4 days in advance, covered, and kept frozen.)

Just before serving, remove the dish from the freezer, allow to soften for a few minutes, then drag the tines of a fork across the surface of the granita to lighten its texture and break up any large frozen lumps. The consistency should be light, frosty, and granular, not much different from that of a snow cone or shaved ice.

Serve the granita in large martini or wine glasses, each garnished with a sprig of fresh mint.

VARIATIONS AND SUGGESTIONS:

This recipe can also be prepared in a creamier and smoother sorbet form, by processing the frozen granita in a food processor fitted with a metal blade. (It may be necessary to do this in several batches.) Process the mixture for about 2 minutes, until it is smooth and creamy, then refreeze until ready to serve. Sorbet yield: about 4 1/2 cups.

NUTRITIONAL ANALYSIS PER SERVING:
Calories: 203 • Protein: 0.85 gram • Carbohydrates: 41.8 grams • Fiber: 0.406 gram • Fat: Total: 0.272 gram • Saturated: 0.051 gram • Cholesterol: 0 • Sodium: 128 milligrams

The Dangers in Doing Public Service Announcements

One would think, from seeing Cher on the silver screen or in a TV movie, that the behind-the-scenes making of a film would run pretty smoothly. Quite the contrary! Several years ago, Cher was asked to do a public service announcement hailing the safety benefits of wearing helmets while riding motorcycles. The shoot was to be set up at her home, where she would sit on her Harley and make the announcement. For a makeshift photography studio, the camera crew set up their cameras and lighting equipment in Cher's garage, where the motorcycle would be positioned.

Meanwhile, Cher was in the house with her hair, makeup, and wardrobe people, being prepared for the filming. When I heard Cher emerging from her bedroom, decked out in a biker jacket and leather chaps, and with a bandana wrapped around her head, I left the kitchen to watch the filming. The multitude of lights came on and the camera was readied. No one could have imagined what was about to happen.

As Cher took her position over the gleaming motorcycle, the director ordered silence while she delivered her lines. Film rolling, Cher had spoken about two words when the automatic sprinkler system in her garage went off, showering water over her and all the film equipment! In seconds, the once serene set became a beehive of activity as crew frantically tried to rescue their gear. Moments later, fire trucks came from all directions as the sprinklers continued to shower the garage.

My boss was soaked. As it turned out, the heat from the lights had triggered the sprinkler system. The filming was postponed, but not before some very tense moments.

Cher's Guidelines to Being "Lean and Clean"

1. Never wait until your body has hunger pains; eat every 3 to 4 hours. (If you're on the go, pack small snacks in little plastic bags or containers so you're not tempted by fast food.)
2. Every time you eat, be sure to combine protein (skinless chicken, turkey, seafood, beans, low-fat cottage cheese) with complex carbohydrates (bread, pasta, potatoes, rice, vegetables). This slows the body's absorption of the carbohydrate and helps to maintain a more even blood sugar level.
3. Choose protein sources that are low in fat.
4. Choose as carbohydrates predominantly fiber-rich vegetables and fruits. Limit starchy carbohydrates and avoid processed junk food, like chips and candy.
5. Limit your fat intake to monounsaturated oils (liquid vegetable oils). Avoid saturated fats (the "hard" fat, mostly found in meats and the skin of poultry).
6. Drink six to eight 8-ounce glasses of water each day.
7. Always involve yourself in some physical cardiovascular activity. Exercise is just as important as how you eat.
8. Keep your meals colorful, with lots of variety in fruits, vegetables, and beans.
9. Remember that a little healthful fat is not an enemy. It slows the absorption of other foods and helps to suppress hunger pangs.
10. Accept your failures and then let them go. There is nothing more damaging than guilt when you are trying your best to do something good for yourself. Move on.

Cher's 10-Day Meal Plan

Cher has one secret to her lifestyle of health and fitness—commitment! Her commitment to eating right and working out keeps her looking her best, not to mention feeling great. She is a hard-working woman who, like many of us in the nineties, leads a life with a demanding schedule and hectic pace. Through my cooking and a good exercise program, Cher has been able to keep fit and feel more confident.

Cooking for Cher over the past eight years has provided me with a wonderful opportunity to work with her sports trainers, doctors, and nutritionists. And although many of them hold conflicting theories on nutrition, I have formulated basic guidelines to help develop this meal plan, which has really worked for Cher in maintaining a lean body.

A few facts to keep in mind: Food can affect our bodies like a drug. When we eat food, it has an effect. Food causes the body's metabolism and blood sugar level to rise. When we starve ourselves in an effort to lose weight, even the smallest amount of food can have huge effects on the body, because the body is not receiving all of its daily requirements, and stores everything it can in fat. The ideal meal plan provides our bodies with small amounts of food throughout the day, keeping the blood sugar level more constant and eliminating the need for the body to store as much in fat.

This is the meal plan I follow for Cher when she wants to get her leanest, and protein is that building block to lean muscle mass. Whether she is preparing for a movie, photo shoot, or music video, this is how Cher keeps looking so great. Cher and I refer to this type of eating as "clean eating." In order to be lean, she must eat clean.

The backbone to the meal plan is to take in more protein (such as egg whites, skinless chicken, turkey, and seafood) while reducing the amount of carbohydrates (such as bread, pasta, potatoes, and rice). Why? Because the body stores as fat carbohydrates not used immediately, while proteins are utilized by the body much more slowly, maintaining a more level blood sugar level throughout the day.

Note that this meal plan is specifically tailored to Cher's dietary needs, based on her own weight, age, fitness level, and other nutritional considerations. Obviously, everyone's body is unique and reacts differently to any weight-management plan, so we do not guarantee any specific results here. Those wishing to follow a dietary plan should consult a physician or nutritionist to determine the proper plan for their specific needs.

DAY ONE
BREAKFAST:
3-egg white omelet with spinach, ¼ cup garbanzo beans, 3 slices of tomato

LUNCH:
1 cup Slim Greek Tuna Salad (page 76), without the olives, over mixed lettuce
    greens; ¼ whole-grain pita pocket bread, ¼ of an avocado

DINNER:
4 ounces Grilled Tuna and Papaya-Mint Salsa (page 82), ¼ cup Black-Eyed
    Pea Salad (page 43), ½ of a grilled zucchini.

NUTRITIONAL ANALYSIS FOR DAY ONE:
Calories: 1058 • Protein: 118 grams • Carbohydrates: 21 grams • Fiber: 4.7 grams • Fat: Total: 29 grams
• Cholesterol: 96 milligrams • Sodium: 1201 milligrams

DAY TWO
BREAKFAST:
1 cup cooked oatmeal or Cream of Wheat with 2 hard-boiled egg whites

LUNCH:
A 4-ounce Barbecue Chicken Burger (page 116), using no-oil barbecue sauce,
    1 cup Spicy Corn Chowder (page 56), ¼ avocado

DINNER:
1 cup Beef Stew and Vegetables (page 125), over ¾ cup baked spaghetti squash

NUTRITIONAL ANALYSIS FOR DAY TWO:
Calories: 1252 • Protein: 104 grams • Carbohydrates: 107 grams • Fiber: 21 grams • Fat: Total: 44.5
grams • Cholesterol: 258 milligrams • Sodium: 2013 milligrams

DAY THREE
BREAKFAST:
1 slice whole-grain toast with 2 teaspoons all-fruit jam, ½ cup low-fat cottage
    cheese, ½ grapefruit or 4 ounces grapefruit juice

LUNCH:

4 ounces Grilled Tuna and ½ cup Papaya-Mint Salsa (page 82), or 3
Spinach-Carrot Rolls (page 158), 3 slices of tomato

DINNER:

4 ounces Fajita Skirt Steak (page 129), 1 cup grilled onions and peppers,
prepared using only cooking spray, 1 corn tortilla, chopped lettuce, and salsa

NUTRITIONAL ANALYSIS FOR DAY THREE:
Calories: 1031 • Protein: 99 grams • Carbohydrates: 99.7 grams • Fiber: 21 grams • Fat: Total: 29.5
grams • Cholesterol: 141 milligrams • Sodium: 1372 milligrams

DAY FOUR

BREAKFAST:

2-egg-white omelet with ½ cup low-fat cottage cheese, 1 slice whole-grain
toast with 2 teaspoons all-fruit jam

LUNCH:

1 cup Turkey Chili (page 104), 1 cup Spinach-Feta Salad with Apples and
Roasted Sunflower Seeds (page 66) or 1 cup steamed broccoli

DINNER:

1 Chicken Rollatini with Sun-Dried Tomatoes (page 112), ¾ cup baked
spaghetti squash with herbs

NUTRITIONAL ANALYSIS FOR DAY FOUR:
Calories: 997 • Protein: 97.8 grams • Carbohydrates: 76.4 grams • Fiber: 15 grams • Fat: Total: 34.4
grams • Cholesterol: 210 milligrams • Sodium: 2232 milligrams

DAY FIVE

BREAKFAST:

1 cup cooked oatmeal, 2 hard-boiled egg whites

LUNCH:

A 4-ounce Elijah's Mustard-Caper Chicken Burger (page 118), 1 cup Greek
Tomato-Feta Salad (page 38)

DINNER:

4 ounces Salmon en Papillote (page 83), ½ cup Carrot-Lemon Purée (page
160), 1 cup steamed asparagus

NUTRITIONAL ANALYSIS FOR DAY FIVE:
Calories: 1159 • Protein: 99 grams • Carbohydrates: 99 grams • Fiber: 25 grams • Fat: Total: 43.5 grams • Cholesterol: 228.3 milligrams • Sodium: 1747 milligrams

DAY SIX

BREAKFAST:

3 scrambled egg whites with fresh herbs, ¼ of an avocado, 1 small apple

LUNCH:

1½ cups Salade Niçoise with 4 ounces of grilled tuna (page 74), omitting the olives

DINNER:

¾ cup Pork, Hominy, Green Chile Stew (page 131), 1 cup Cut Grilled Vegetables (page 156)

NUTRITIONAL ANALYSIS FOR DAY SIX:
Calories: 1027 • Protein: 104 grams • Carbohydrates: 75 grams • Fiber: 14 grams • Fat: Total: 35.5 grams • Cholesterol: 164 milligrams • Sodium: 1058 milligrams

DAY SEVEN

BREAKFAST:

1 cup cooked oatmeal with 2 hard-boiled egg whites

LUNCH:

2 Cajun Swordfish Brochettes (page 85), ¼ cup Black-Eyed Pea Salad, ½ of a grilled zucchini

DINNER:

4 ounces Tandoori Chicken Brochettes (page 110), ⅓ cup Spicy Hummus (page 40), 1 cup Spinach-Feta Salad with Apples and Roasted Sunflower Seeds (page 66)

NUTRITIONAL ANALYSIS FOR DAY SEVEN:
Calories: 1290 • Protein: 132 grams • Carbohydrates: 125 grams • Fiber: 19 grams • Fat: Total: 27 grams • Cholesterol: 143 milligrams • Sodium: 1783 milligrams

DAY EIGHT

BREAKFAST:

4 ounces fresh-squeezed grapefruit juice, 1 slice whole-grain toast with 2 teaspoons all-fruit jam, ½ cup low-fat cottage cheese

LUNCH:

4 ounces Chilled Shrimp and Cocktail Sauce (page 49), 1 cup Shredded
   Vegetable Salad with Low-Fat Blue Cheese Dressing (page 69)

DINNER:

1 grilled chicken breast, 1 cup grilled vegetables, $1/3$ cup garbanzo beans

NUTRITIONAL ANALYSIS FOR DAY EIGHT:
Calories: 1074 • Protein: 103 grams • Carbohydrates: 128 grams • Fiber: 19 grams • Fat: Total: 19.5
grams • Cholesterol: 280 milligrams • Sodium: 2012 milligrams

DAY NINE

BREAKFAST:

1 cup cooked Cream of Wheat with 2 hard-boiled egg whites

LUNCH:

4 ounces grilled fresh halibut, 1 cup Potato-Leek Soup (page 61), 1 cup
   steamed mixed vegetables with a mixture of balsamic vinegar and Dijon
   mustard

DINNER:

6 chicken or shrimp wontons from recipe for Oriental Wontons and Dipping
   Sauce (page 51), 1 cup stir-fried vegetables seasoned with rice wine vinegar
   and a few drops of soy sauce, 2 Spinach-Carrot Rolls (page 158)

NUTRITIONAL ANALYSIS FOR DAY NINE:
Calories: 1153 • Protein: 86 grams • Carbohydrates: 177 grams • Fiber: 22.4 grams • Fat: Total: 14.3
grams • Cholesterol: 106 milligrams • Sodium: 2800 milligrams

DAY TEN

BREAKFAST:

3-egg-white omelet with $1/4$ cup spinach, 1 green onion, and $1/4$ cup
   mushrooms; $1/4$ cup low-fat cottage cheese

LUNCH:

A taco salad consisting of: 4 ounces seasoned and browned ground turkey on a
   bed of 1 cup shredded lettuce, $1/4$ cup Unfried Refried Beans (page 176),
   and salsa

DINNER:

4 ounces Crisp Sea Scallops in Spicy Roasted Red Pepper Sauce (page 87),
   1 cup Cut Grilled Vegetables (page 156), ¼ cup Black-Eyed Pea Salad (page
   43)

NUTRITIONAL ANALYSIS FOR DAY TEN:
Calories: 1302 • Protein: 131.8 grams • Carbohydrates: 97.5 grams • Fiber: 20 grams • Fat: Total: 42.8
grams • Cholesterol: 307 milligrams • Sodium: 2109 milligrams

Menus for Special Occasions

Here are menus from some of the special occasions celebrated in Cher's home throughout the year. They include many recipes appearing in this cookbook that have become family favorites. Obviously, some of the recipes are not low in fat, but we believe that it is good to indulge sometimes.

Included in these menus are familiar foods for which most people have their own favorite recipes, like roast turkey, potato salad, or pecan pie; no recipes for such dishes are given in this book. Use these menu suggestions as a guide to making your own special occasions worth celebrating.

CHRISTMAS

*W*hether in the snowy mountains of Aspen or on the
balmy coast of Miami, we
have always spent Christmas in special places. Preparations for Christmas dinner usually involve a joint family gathering in the kitchen, with
each person making a favorite recipe. With all the cooking going on, I
save time by preparing the yams and cookie dough a day or two in
advance; the ham is store-bought. On Christmas Day, Cher serves
everything in her festive Christmas china—Santa's sack for the yams,
reindeer bowls for the ambrosia, and a Christmas tree platter for the
ham. Later in the evening, baking and decorating gingerbread cookies
make a nice end to a full day in the kitchen.

Cher's Ambrosia (page 45)

Honeybaked ham

Holiday Spice Whipped Yams (page 164)

Chastity's Italian Spinach and Onions (page 153)

Gingerbread cookies

THANKSGIVING

*E*veryone has favorite recipes for Thanksgiving, especially for roast turkey, mashed potatoes, and pies. And even though this holiday is not the best time to watch your waistline, you can cut some calories by eating the turkey without the skin, preparing mashed potatoes with low-fat buttermilk, and ending the meal with Pumpkin Flan (page 188).

Thanksgiving is a time to appreciate the bounty of food for which we are so fortunate. Like colorful autumn leaves, this is a meal that celebrates the season—spinach salad with the last of the apple harvest, roast turkey with savory corn bread dressing, tart cranberries, and sweet pies.

Spinach-Feta Salad with Apples and
Roasted Sunflower Seeds (page 66)

Roast turkey

Georgia's Corn Bread Dressing (page 167)

Mashed potatoes

No-Fat Homemade Gravy (page 119)

Cherry-Lemon Cranberry Sauce (page 48)

Pumpkin and pecan pies

APRÈS-SKI PARTY

*I*n the winter, whenever we are in the mountains and everyone goes skiing, Cher loves to throw an après-ski party. While the fireplace warms all the chilly toes, lively conversation fills the air about the favorite ski run of the day or the mogul that almost broke someone's leg. So when the troops come stomping in, this is the perfect menu to warm body and soul—a bubbling pot of chili, steaming cornbread muffins, and a toast with sparkling cider!

Sparkling apple cider

Spicy Corn Chowder (page 56)

Mexican Corn Bread (page 170)

Turkey Chili (page 104)

Chocolate Brownies (page 185)

FOURTH OF JULY BARBECUE

*A*t the height of summer, we celebrate Fourth of July by inviting family and friends for a casual backyard barbecue. In the morning, Cher stirs up her favorite baked beans, while I prepare my crisp dill coleslaw. Use your favorite potato salad recipe, and if you are short on time, you can always use store-bought coleslaw, potato salad, and barbecued chicken.

Dill Coleslaw (page 42)

Red-skin potato salad

Cher's BBQ Baked Beans (page 177)

Grilled barbecue chicken

Brownie Ice-Cream Sandwiches (see variations and suggestions for Chocolate Brownies recipe, page 135)

BABY SHOWERS

*O*ccasionally, Cher will throw a baby shower for a special girl-friend who is expecting. The shower is usually a large gathering of women and children; we like to have lighter food, buffet-style, so that all the guests can help themselves while watching the opening of gifts. I usually prepare a platter of fresh sliced fruit, which may include melon, berries, or whatever fruit is in season. After the gifts are opened, I like to serve warm cobbler for dessert.

Fresh fruit platter

Cher's Tuna Pasta Salad (page 78)

Cold Potato-Leek Soup (page 61)

Nectarine-Blueberry Cobbler (page 190)

BUSINESS MEETINGS

*M*any people won-
der why I am so
busy at Cher's
home. What they don't realize is that Cher runs her production company out of her house, so there are often business meetings that take
place over lunch or dinner. Obviously, most of the meetings are not
appropriate for sit-down meals, so I mainly prepare finger food, to
which people can help themselves. This is a typical menu for these
meetings.

Chilled Shrimp and Cocktail Sauce (page 49)

Crudités of jicama, radicchio, fennel, and yellow bell
pepper; Cher's Ranch Dressing (page 31)

Barbecue chicken skewers

Cut Grilled Vegetables (page 156)

Assorted cookies

BIRTHDAY PARTIES

*B*irthdays are usually a pretty big deal at Cher's house. Preparations include filling the dining room with helium balloons, while monstrous birthday cakes are delivered to the door. We've had birthday cakes designed with everything imaginable—a replica of an album cover, scenes from Cher's movies, and even an Academy Award Oscar! We don't pretend these cakes are low-fat!

Whenever there is a birthday, Cher loves to have this chicken for dinner. Actually, she asks for it so much for every birthday party that guests think it is the only dish I make!

Chilled Asparagus with Balsamic Vinaigrette (page 33)

Olive Tapenade Chicken (page 95)

Rustic Grilled Tomato Sauce and Pasta (page 142)

Birthday cake and ice cream

Resources:
Finding What You Need

Here is a helpful list of sources where you may be able to find specific food products or kitchen equipment used in *Cooking for Cher*. Many of these companies have mail-order catalogues or they can provide you with the necessary information on distributors of their products in your area. Also included are some noteworthy products that do not appear in my recipes but are favorite products that Cher and I really like.

GRACE'S MARKETPLACE
1237 Third Avenue
New York, NY 10021
(212) 737-0600 (local number)
(888) GRACES 1 (toll-free)
www.gracesmkt.com (computer internet on-line address)

Specialty-food products, a large selection of nuts and dried fruits, including the dried cherries that I use, spices, baking extracts, cheeses, deli items, and baked goods. One of my favorite stores in New York.

DEAN & DELUCA
Catalogue Department
P.O. Box 20810
Wichita, KS 67208-6810
(800) 221-7714

Specialty-food and equipment products, deli items, fresh breads, and pastries. They will ship almost anything they carry.

REILY FOODS CO.
P.O. Box 60296
New Orleans, LA 70160
(800) 535-1961

Woody's Cook-in sauce barbecue concentrate, as well as other Cajun food products.

CHEF PAUL PRUDHOMME'S MAGIC SEASONING BLENDS
824 Distributors Row
Harahan, LA 70123
(504) 731-3590 (in Louisiana)
(800) 457-2857 (outside Louisiana)

Cajun blackening seasonings and spices. Call for a catalogue of their products.

VOLCANO ISLAND HONEY COMPANY
Beekeeper: Richard Spiegel
P.O. Box 1709
Honokaa, Hawaii
(808) 775-0806 (phone and fax)

Cher's favorite honey, to put in her tea just before a voice lesson. Rare Hawaiian White Honey is a truly unique "hard" white honey, unheated and unfiltered, with an impeccable flavor. Also beeswax candles. Prices include shipping, but the minimum order must be at least $36. Richard can provide you with a list of stores where their honey can be purchased here on the mainland.

OAKVILLE GROCERY (3 SAN FRANCISCO LOCATIONS)
715 Stanford Shopping Center
Palo Alto, CA 94304
(415) 328-9000

Myriad specialty-food products: olive oil, honey, tea, dressings, Indian spices and marinades, Greek olives, and an amazing wine selection.

WILLIAMS-SONOMA
Mail Order Department
P.O. Box 7456
San Francisco, CA 94120-7456
(800) 541-2233

Catalogue of kitchen cookware, bakeware, tools and utensils, appliances, cookbooks, specialty foods, tableware, and linens. Retail locations can be found in many larger cities across the country.

DISH N' DAT
510 N.W. 11th Avenue
Portland, OR 97209
(503) 279-8946

An excellent selection of kitchen tools and tableware.

COOK'S WAREHOUSE, INC.
7650 Haskell Avenue, Suite A
Van Nuys, CA 91406
(818) 909-9898
(818) 778-6424 (fax)

They carry a complete line of nonstick pots, pans, and skillets.

CHEF'S CATALOG
3215 Commercial Avenue
Northbrook, IL 60062
(800) 338-3232 (24-hour ordering service)

Kitchen equipment of all kinds for the home chef.

SILVER PALATE KITCHENS, INC.
P.O. Box 512
Cresskill, NJ 07626
(201) 568-0110

For information on the entire line of the Silver Palate food products and where they can be purchased in your area. Everything from regular and low-fat salad splashes to delicious sauces, marinades, salsas, chutneys, mustards, and ice-cream toppings.

THE HONEYBAKED HAM CO.
623 S. Brookhurst
Anaheim, CA 92804
(800) 854-5995

Hams, turkeys, and a selection of condiments. Call them for sizes and prices. Every year during the holidays, we order one of these amazing hams. They will ship almost anywhere.

WAX ORCHARDS
22744 Wax Orchard Road, SW
Vashon, WA 98070
(800) 634-6132

Fruit-sweetened, fat-free chocolate fudge sauce (Classic Fudge) and other products. Send a self-addressed stamped envelope for catalogues and recipes.

SOY VAY ENTERPRISES
Mail Order
5969 Hillside Drive
Felton, CA 95018

Sesame teriyaki sauce and Chinese marinade, unlike other brands commercially available.

HOGWASH ENTERPRISES/JOHNNY D'S BARBEQUE CO.
P.O. Box 75
Los Alamitos, CA 90720
(800) BASTE IT

Low-sugar barbecue sauce that will not burn as easily when basting grilled food items. Excellent flavor. Full line of barbecue marinades and bastes for grilling beef, seafood, and poultry.

PENZEYS SPICE HOUSE, LTD
P.O. Box 933
Muskego, WI 53150
(414) 574-0277
(414) 574-0278 (fax)

Mail-order catalogue of spices, herbs, and seasonings. Excellent source for exotic, ethnic spices.

CULINARY INSTITUTE OF AMERICA/CRAIG CLAIBORNE BOOKSTORE
433 Albany Post Road
Hyde Park, NY 12538
(800) 677-6266

Excellent source for all kinds of specialty chef's tools, equipment, and clothing, as well as published culinary material.

SEEDS OF CHANGE
Box 15700, Dept. KG63
Santa Fe, NM 87506-5700
(800) 957-3337

Mail-order catalogue for organic seeds to grow in your own garden. Heirloom, traditional, and hard-to-find varieties of vegetables, herbs, and flowers.

THE CMC COMPANY
P.O. Box 322
Avalon, NJ 08202
(800) CMC-2780

Mexican food products: Masa Harina, canned tomatillos, hot sauces, and spices.

KITCHEN ARTS & LETTERS BOOKSTORE
1435 Lexington Avenue
New York, NY 10128
(212) 876-5550

Index

METRIC EQUIVALENCIES

Liquid and Dry Measure Equivalencies

Customary	Metric
¹/₄ teaspoon	1.25 milliliters
¹/₂ teaspoon	2.5 milliliters
1 teaspoon	5 milliliters
1 tablespoon	15 milliliters
1 fluid ounce	30 milliliters
¹/₄ cup	60 milliliters
¹/₃ cup	80 milliliters
¹/₂ cup	120 milliliters
1 cup	240 milliliters
1 pint (2 cups)	480 milliliters
1 quart (4 cups)	960 milliliters (.96 liter)
1 gallon (4 quarts)	3.84 liters
1 ounce (by weight)	28 grams
¹/₄ pound (4 ounces)	114 grams
1 pound (16 ounces)	454 grams
2.2 pounds	1 kilogram (1000 grams)

Oven-Temperature Equivalencies

Description	°Fahrenheit	°Celsius
Cool	200	90
Very slow	250	120
Slow	300–325	150–160
Moderately slow	325–350	160–180
Moderate	350–375	180–190
Moderately hot	375–400	190–200
Hot	400–450	200–230
Very hot	450–500	230–260